QUICK AND COZY AFGHANS

Everyone loves afghans, but today's busy schedules often limit the time we can devote to crocheting them. So to help you make the most of your stitching minutes, we've gathered the best of our fast and easy patterns into this indispensable volume, Quick and Cozy Afghans.

Whether you need a light wrap or a warm throw, you'll find just the right afghan to suit your decor in one of our four designer sections. In Classic Elegance, we have lush styles in muted colors to accent a distinctive atmosphere. Country Casual features cozy wraps that will give an informal room a relaxed, nostalgic charm. In our Soft and Sweet section, you'll discover a bouquet of delicate coverlets to lend a feminine touch to a bedroom or a tender look to a nursery. And finally, the afghans in Colorful Mix offer a playful collection of bright colors and bold patterns that will please your kids (or the kid in you!).

Gleaned from favorite Leisure Arts leaflets and magazines, these stylish wraps are crocheted using fast, easy techniques that both beginners and experts will enjoy. Basic stitches and simple patterns produce simply dramatic effects, and many of our afghans are worked using a large hook and several strands of yarn held together for beautiful results in no time.

With this treasury of 52 irresistible designs, you can crochet afghans for every room of your home and every member of your family — the quick and easy way!

LEISURE ARTS, INC.
and
OXMOOR HOUSE, INC.

EDITORIAL STAFF

Editor-in-Chief: Anne Van Wagner Childs
Executive Director: Sandra Graham Case
Executive Editor: Susan Frantz Wiles
Publications Director: Carla Bentley
Creative Art Director: Gloria Bearden
Production Art Director: Melinda Stout

PRODUCTION
Managing Editor: Linda Luder
Senior Editor: Sarah J. Green

EDITORIAL
Associate Editor: Linda L. Trimble
Senior Editorial Writer: Terri Leming Davidson
Editorial Writer: Darla Burdette Kelsay
Editorial Associate: Tammi Williamson Bradley
Copy Editor: Laura Lee Weland

ART
Book/Magazine Art Director: Diane M. Ghegan
Senior Production Artist: M. Katherine Yancey
Assistant Production Artist: Brent Jones
Photography Stylists: Christina Tiano, Sondra Daniel,
    and Laura Bushmiaer

BUSINESS STAFF

Publisher: Steve Patterson
Controller: Tom Siebenmorgen
Retail Sales Director: Richard Tignor
Retail Marketing Director: Pam Stebbins
Retail Customer Services Director: Margaret Sweetin
Marketing Manager: Russ Barnett
Executive Director of Marketing and Circulation:
    Guy A. Crossley
Fulfillment Manager: Byron L. Taylor
Print Production Manager: Laura Lockhart
Print Production Coordinator: Nancy Reddick Lister

Quick and Cozy Afghans
from the *Crochet Treasury* series
Published by Leisure Arts, Inc., and Oxmoor House, Inc.

Library of Congress Catalog Number: 94-77962
Hardcover ISBN 0-942237-47-1
Softcover ISBN 0-942237-48-X

TABLE OF CONTENTS

COUNTRY CASUAL

The simple charm of a country home invites us to be at ease — especially when there's always a cozy comforter within reach! The afghans in this wonderful gathering will add a relaxing touch to your family room, a covered porch, or even a Sunday picnic. Quick to crochet in favorite designs such as ripple and mile-a-minute patterns, these nostalgic wraps will warm your home with the leisurely hospitality of yesteryear.

LACY BLOCKS

Although this lacy throw looks like it's fashioned in blocks and then joined, it's actually worked all in one piece using only single, double, and treble crochet stitches. Brushed acrylic yarn gives feathery softness to the delicate spiderweb pattern.

Finished Size: Approximately 50" x 74"

MATERIALS
Worsted Weight Brushed Acrylic Yarn,
approximately:
36^{1}/$_{2}$ ounces, (1,040 grams, 2,815 yards)
Crochet hook, size H (5.00 mm) **or** size needed for
gauge

GAUGE: 15 dc and 7^{1}/$_{2}$ rows = 4"

Ch 185 **loosely**.
Row 1: Dc in fourth ch from hook and in each ch across:
183 sts.
Row 2 (Right side)**:** Ch 3 **(counts as first dc, now and throughout)**, turn; dc in next 2 dc, ★ ch 1, skip next dc, dc in next 15 dc; repeat from ★ across to last 4 dc, ch 1, skip next dc, dc in last 3 dc: 171 dc.
Note: Loop a short piece of yarn around any stitch to mark last row as **right** side.
Row 3: Ch 3, turn; dc in next 2 dc, ★ ch 1, skip next ch, dc in next dc, (ch 1, skip next dc, dc in next dc) 7 times; repeat from ★ across to last 3 dc, ch 1, skip next ch, dc in last 3 dc: 88 ch-1 sps.
Row 4: Ch 3, turn; dc in next 2 dc, ★ ch 1, skip next ch, dc in next dc, (dc in next ch-1 sp, dc in next dc) 7 times; repeat from ★ across to last 3 dc, ch 1, skip next ch, dc in last 3 dc: 171 dc.
Row 5: Ch 3, turn; dc in next 2 dc, ★ ch 1, skip next ch, dc in next 15 dc; repeat from ★ across to last 3 dc, ch 1, skip next ch, dc in last 3 dc.
Row 6: Ch 3, turn; dc in next 2 dc, ★ ch 1, skip next ch, dc in next 3 dc, ch 3, (skip next dc, tr in next dc) 4 times, ch 3, skip next dc, dc in next 3 dc; repeat from ★ across to last 3 dc, ch 1, skip next ch, dc in last 3 dc: 72 dc and 44 tr.

Row 7: Ch 3, turn; dc in next 2 dc, ★ ch 1, skip next ch, dc in next 3 dc, ch 3, sc in next 4 tr, ch 3, dc in next 3 dc; repeat from ★ across to last 3 dc, ch 1, skip next ch, dc in last 3 dc.
Rows 8-10: Ch 3, turn; dc in next 2 dc, ★ ch 1, skip next ch, dc in next 3 dc, ch 3, sc in next 4 sc, ch 3, dc in next 3 dc; repeat from ★ across to last 3 dc, ch 1, skip next ch, dc in last 3 dc.
Row 11: Ch 3, turn; dc in next 2 dc, ★ ch 1, skip next ch, dc in next 3 dc, ch 1, (tr in next sc, ch 1) 4 times, dc in next 3 dc; repeat from ★ across to last 3 dc, ch 1, skip next ch, dc in last 3 dc.
Row 12: Ch 3, turn; dc in next 2 dc, ★ ch 1, skip next ch, dc in next 3 dc, dc in next ch-1 sp, (dc in next tr, dc in next ch-1 sp) 4 times, dc in next 3 dc; repeat from ★ across to last 3 dc, ch 1, skip next ch, dc in last 3 dc: 171 dc.
Row 13: Ch 3, turn; dc in next 2 dc, ★ ch 1, skip next ch, dc in next 15 dc; repeat from ★ across to last 3 dc, ch 1, skip next ch, dc in last 3 dc.
Rows 14-136: Repeat Rows 3-13, 11 times; then repeat Rows 3 and 4 once **more**: 171 dc.
Row 137: Ch 3, turn; dc in each dc and in each ch-1 sp across; do **not** finish off: 183 dc.

EDGING

Rnd 1: Ch 1, turn; sc in each dc across; working in end of rows, 3 sc in first row, work 270 sc evenly spaced across to last row, 3 sc in last row; working in free loops of beginning ch **(Fig. 27b, page 124)**, work 183 sc evenly spaced across; working in end of rows, work 3 sc in first row, work 270 sc evenly spaced across to last row, 3 sc in last row; join with slip st to first sc: 918 sc.
Rnd 2: Ch 1, do **not** turn; ★ sc in next sc, ch 4, sc in third ch from hook, ch 2, skip next 2 sc; repeat from ★ around; join with slip st to first sc, finish off.

ALL-AMERICAN AFGHAN

Stripes of red, white, and blue make a striking all-American showing on this simple afghan. Worked with easy double crochet stitches and two strands of yarn held together, the tweed look is created by simply alternating the color combinations.

Finished Size: Approximately 48" x 66"

MATERIALS
Worsted Weight Yarn, approximately:
MC (Dark Blue) - 39 ounces,
    (1,110 grams, 2,450 yards)
Color A (Dark Red) - 8 ounces,
    (230 grams, 505 yards)
Color B (White) - 8 ounces,
    (230 grams, 505 yards)
Crochet hook, size P (10.00 mm) **or** size needed for
gauge

Note: Entire Afghan is worked holding two strands of
yarn together.

GAUGE: 8 dc and 4 rows = 4"

With one strand of MC and one strand of Color A,
ch 94 **loosely**.
Row 1 (Right side): Dc in fourth ch from hook and in
each ch across changing to 2 strands of MC in last dc
(Fig. 28, page 124): 92 sts.
Note: Do **not** cut old color. Carry yarn loosely along edge
and work over loose strands when working Rnd 1 of
Edging.
Row 2: Ch 3 **(counts as first dc, now and throughout),**
turn; dc in next dc and in each st across changing to one
strand of MC and one strand of Color B in last dc: 92 dc.
Row 3: Ch 3, turn; dc in next dc and in each dc across
changing to one strand of MC and one strand of Color A
in last dc.
Row 4: Ch 3, turn; dc in next dc and in each dc across
changing to 2 strands of MC in last dc.
Row 5: Ch 3, turn; dc in next dc and in each dc across
changing to one strand of MC and one strand of Color B in
last dc.
Row 6: Ch 3, turn; dc in next dc and in each dc across
changing to one strand of MC and one strand of Color A
in last dc.
Row 7: Ch 3, turn; dc in next dc and in each dc across
changing to 2 strands of MC in last dc.
Rows 8-64: Repeat Rows 5-7, 19 times; at end of Row 64,
do **not** finish off, cut Color A and Color B **only**.

EDGING
Rnd 1: Ch 1, turn; 3 sc in first dc, sc in next dc and in
each dc across to last dc, 3 sc in last dc; work 2 sc in end of
each row across; working in free loops of beginning ch
(Fig. 27b, page 124), 3 sc in first ch, sc in next 90 chs,
3 sc in next ch; work 2 sc in end of each row across; join
with slip st to first sc: 448 sc.
Rnd 2: Ch 3, do **not** turn; 3 dc in next sc, ★ dc in each sc
across to next corner sc, 3 dc in corner sc; repeat from
★ 2 times **more**, dc in each sc across; join with slip st to
first dc, finish off.

HERB GARDEN

Rich shades of green give the strips of this mile-a-minute afghan the appearance of a lush Victorian herb garden. The eye-catching pattern is created by working a wavy border around the openwork centers of the strips.

Finished Size: Approximately 50" x 65"

MATERIALS
Worsted Weight Yarn, approximately:
Color A (Beige) - 8 ounces, (230 grams, 525 yards)
Color B (Green) - 20 ounces,
(570 grams, 1,315 yards)
Color C (Dark Green) - 8 ounces,
(230 grams, 525 yards)
Crochet hook, size K (6.50 mm) **or** size needed for
gauge
Yarn needle

GAUGE: 12 sc and 14 rows = 4"
One Strip = 6¹/4" wide

STRIP (Make 8)
CENTER
With Color B, ch 6; join with slip st to form a ring.
Row 1 (Wrong side): Ch 3 **(counts as first dc, now and throughout)**, (2 dc, ch 2, 3 dc) in ring: 6 dc.
Note: Loop a short piece of yarn around any stitch to mark last row as **wrong** side and bottom edge.
Rows 2-89: Ch 3, turn; (2 dc, ch 2, 2 dc) in next ch-2 sp, skip next 2 dc, dc in last dc.
Finish off.

BORDER
Rnd 1: With **right** side facing, beginning at bottom edge and working in end of rows, join Color A with slip st in first row; ch 1, (sc, ch 3, sc) in same row (first corner), 3 sc in next row, 2 sc in each row across to last row, (sc, ch 3, sc) in last row (corner); working across Row 89, 2 sc in next ch-2 sp; working in end of rows, (sc, ch 3, sc) in first row (corner), 2 sc in each row across to last 2 rows, 3 sc in next row, (sc, ch 3, sc) in last row (corner); 2 sc in beginning ring; join with slip st to Back Loop Only of first sc **(Fig. 26, page 124)**, finish off: 362 sc.
Note: Work in Back Loops Only throughout.
Rnd 2: With **right** side facing and bottom edge to the right, join Color C with slip st in ch-3 sp of first corner; ch 1, 5 sc in same sp, † sc in next 2 sc, hdc in next sc, dc in next sc, 3 tr in next sc, dc in next sc, hdc in next sc,

★ sc in next sc, hdc in next sc, dc in next sc, 3 tr in next sc, dc in next sc, hdc in next sc; repeat from ★ 27 times **more**, sc in next 2 sc, 5 sc in next corner ch-3 sp, sc in next 4 sc †, 5 sc in next corner ch-3 sp, repeat from † to † once; join with slip st to first sc, finish off: 498 sts.
Note #1: To **decrease**, pull up a loop in next 2 sts, YO and draw through all 3 loops on hook.
Note #2: To **double decrease**, pull up a loop in next 3 sts, YO and draw through all 4 loops on hook.
Rnd 3: With **right** side facing and bottom edge to the right, join Color A with slip st in center sc of first corner; ch 1, (sc, ch 2, sc) in same st, † sc in next 3 sc, decrease, sc in next 2 sts, 3 sc in next tr, sc in next 2 sts, ★ double decrease, sc in next 2 sts, 3 sc in next tr, sc in next 2 sts; repeat from ★ 27 times **more**, decrease, sc in next 3 sc, (sc, ch 2, sc) in next sc, sc in next 8 sc †, (sc, ch 2, sc) in next corner sc, repeat from † to † once; join with slip st to first sc, finish off: 510 sts.
Note: To **tr decrease** (uses next 3 sts), ★ YO twice, insert hook in **next** st, YO and pull up a loop, (YO and draw through 2 loops on hook) twice; repeat from ★ 2 times **more**, YO and draw through all 4 loops on hook.
Rnd 4: With **right** side facing and bottom edge to the right, join Color B with slip st in first corner ch-2 sp; ch 4, tr in same sp, † tr in next 3 sc, tr decrease, ★ dc in next sc, hdc in next sc, sc in next sc, hdc in next sc, dc in next sc, tr decrease; repeat from ★ 28 times **more**, tr in next 3 sc, (2 tr, ch 3, 2 tr) in next corner ch-2 sp, tr in next 10 sc †, (2 tr, ch 3, 2 tr) in next corner ch-2 sp, repeat from † to † once, 2 tr in same corner sp as beginning ch-4, ch 3; join with slip st to top of beginning ch-4, do **not** finish off: 410 sts.
Rnd 5: Ch 1, sc in same st and in each st across to next corner ch-3 sp, 3 sc in corner sp, ★ sc in each st across to next corner ch-3 sp, 3 sc in corner sp; repeat from ★ around; join with slip st to first sc, finish off.

ASSEMBLY
With **wrong** side of two Strips together, bottom edges at the same end and using Color B, whipstitch Strips together working in inside loops and beginning in center sc of first corner and ending in center sc of next corner **(Fig. 29a, page 125)**.
Join remaining Strips in same manner, always working from the same direction.

PLAIN AND SIMPLE

As plain and simple as country living, this traditional ripple afghan gets its casual look from soft country-blue yarn. The cozy throw works up quickly because it's fashioned holding two strands of worsted weight yarn together.

Finished Size: Approximately 54" x 74"

MATERIALS

Worsted Weight Yarn, approximately:
53 ounces, (1,510 grams, 3,330 yards)
Crochet hook, size N (9.00 mm) **or** size needed for gauge

Note: Entire Afghan is worked holding two strands of yarn together.

GAUGE: 8 dc and 4 rows = 4"

Ch 135 **loosely**.

Row 1 (Right side)**:** Dc in fourth ch from hook and in each ch across: 133 sts.

Note: To **decrease** (uses next 3 dc), YO, insert hook in **next** dc, YO and pull up a loop, YO and draw through 2 loops on hook, YO, skip **next** dc, insert hook in **next** dc, YO and pull up a loop, YO and draw through 2 loops on hook, YO and draw through all 3 loops on hook (**counts as one dc**).

Row 2: Ch 4 (**counts as first dc plus ch 1**), turn; (dc, ch 1) twice in same dc, (skip next dc, dc in next dc) 3 times, skip next dc, decrease, (skip next dc, dc in next dc) 3 times, ch 1, skip next dc, ★ (dc, ch 1, dc, ch 1, dc) in each of next 2 dc, ch 1, (skip next dc, dc in next dc) 3 times, skip next dc, decrease, (skip next dc, dc in next dc) 3 times, ch 1, skip next dc; repeat from ★ 5 times **more**, (dc, ch 1, dc, ch 1, dc) in next ch.

Row 3: Ch 3, turn; dc in each ch-1 sp and in each dc across: 133 sts.

Repeat Rows 2 and 3 until Afghan measures approximately 74", ending by working Row 3.

Finish off.

FLOWER PATCH

A garden of flowers blooms within the triangle motifs of this charming throw. The airy triangles are worked up quickly using double strands of yarn, then whipstitched together. Delightful star motifs fill in the intersections, completing the pretty look.

Finished Size: Approximately 45" x 54"

MATERIALS
Worsted Weight Yarn, approximately:
MC (Ecru) - 25 ounces, (710 grams, 1,645 yards)
Color A (Pink) - 7 ounces, (200 grams, 460 yards)
Color B (Green) - 7 ounces, (200 grams, 460 yards)
Crochet hook, size N (9.00 mm) **or** size needed for gauge
Yarn needle

Note: Entire Afghan is worked holding two strands of yarn together.

GAUGE: One Motif = 5¹/2"
(from point to opposite straight edge)

MOTIF #1 (Make 44)
With MC, ch 5; join with slip st to form a ring.
Rnd 1 (Right side)**:** Ch 4 **(counts as first dc plus ch 1, now and throughout)**, (dc in ring, ch 1) 11 times; join with slip st to first dc: 12 ch-1 sps.
Note: Loop a short piece of yarn around any stitch to mark last round as **right** side.
Rnd 2: Slip st in first ch-1 sp, ch 4, (tr, ch 5, tr) in next ch-1 sp, ch 1, ★ (dc in next ch-1 sp, ch 1) 3 times, (tr, ch 5, tr) in next ch-1 sp, ch 1; repeat from ★ once **more**, (dc in next ch-1 sp, ch 1) twice; join with slip st to first dc: 15 sps.
Rnd 3: Slip st in first ch-1 sp, ch 1, sc in same sp, ch 1, (sc, ch 1, sc, ch 3, sc, ch 1, sc) in next ch-5 sp, ch 1, ★ (sc in next ch-1 sp, ch 1) 4 times, (sc, ch 1, sc, ch 3, sc, ch 1, sc) in next ch-5 sp, ch 1; repeat from ★ once **more**, (sc in next ch-1 sp, ch 1) 3 times; join with slip st to first sc, finish off.

MOTIF #2 (Make 11)
With Color A, work same as Motif #1.

MOTIF #3 (Make 11)
With Color B, work same as Motif #1.

MOTIF #4 (Make 11)
With MC, ch 5; join with slip st to form a ring.
Rnd 1 (Right side)**:** Ch 4, (dc in ring, ch 1) 11 times; join with slip st to first dc, finish off: 12 ch-1 sps.
Note: Mark last round as **right** side.
Rnd 2: With **right** side facing, join Color A with slip st in any ch-1 sp; ch 4, (tr, ch 5, tr) in next ch-1 sp, ch 1, ★ (dc in next ch-1 sp, ch 1) 3 times, (tr, ch 5, tr) in next ch-1 sp, ch 1; repeat from ★ once **more**, (dc in next ch-1 sp, ch 1) twice; join with slip st to first dc, finish off: 15 sps.
Rnd 3: With **right** side facing, join MC with slip st in ch-1 sp to left of joining; ch 1, sc in same sp, ch 1, (sc, ch 1, sc, ch 3, sc, ch 1, sc) in next ch-5 sp, ch 1, ★ (sc in next ch-1 sp, ch 1) 4 times, (sc, ch 1, sc, ch 3, sc, ch 1, sc) in next ch-5 sp, ch 1; repeat from ★ once **more**, (sc in next ch-1 sp, ch 1) 3 times; join with slip st to first sc, finish off.

MOTIF #5 (Make 11)
Work same as Motif #4, substituting Color B for Color A on Rnd 2.

ASSEMBLY
With **wrong** sides together and working through inside loops, whipstitch 11 Motifs into 8 horizontal strips **(Fig. 29a, page 125)**, referring to Placement Chart **(Fig. 15, page 120)** and leaving ch-3 sps of each corner unjoined.
Join strips in same manner.

STAR MOTIF (Make 32)
With MC, ch 4; join with slip st to form a ring, ch 1, sc in ring, ch 2; with **right** side facing and working in intersection of 6 Motifs, slip st in any joining, ch 2, ★ sc in ring, ch 2, slip st in next joining, ch 2; repeat from ★ 4 times **more**; join with slip st to first sc **(Fig. 16, page 120)**, finish off.

EDGING

Rnd 1: With **right** side facing, join MC with slip st in sc to left of corner ch-3 sp of any Motif; ch 1, sc in same st, ★ sc in each ch-1 sp and in each sc across to next ch-3 sp, 2 sc in each ch-3 sp; repeat from ★ around; join with slip st to first sc.

Rnd 2: Ch 1, hdc in same st, ch 1; working from **left** to **right**, skip next sc, ★ work reverse hdc in next sc *(Figs. 18a-d, page 121)*, ch 1, skip next sc; repeat from ★ around; join with slip st to first hdc, finish off.

COUNTRY FISHERMAN

*A country home just wouldn't be complete without this handsome
throw! The classic fisherman pattern features alternating diamond and
popcorn panels bordered by traditional cables. It works up quickly
because you crochet it holding two strands of worsted weight yarn.*

Finished Size: Approximately 50" x 74"

MATERIALS
Worsted Weight Yarn, approximately:
    78 ounces, (2,220 grams, 4,905 yards)
Crochet hook, size N (9.00 mm) **or** size needed for
    gauge

Note: Entire Afghan is worked holding two strands of
    yarn together.

GAUGE: 8 dc and 4 rows = 4"

CABLE PANEL (Make 2)
Ch 151 **loosely.**

Row 1 (Right side): Dc in fourth ch from hook and in
each ch across: 149 sts.

Note: Loop a short piece of yarn around any stitch to mark
last row as **right** side.

Row 2: Ch 3 **(counts as first dc, now and throughout),**
turn; dc in next dc and in each st across.

Row 3: Ch 1, turn; sc in first dc, ch 3 **loosely,** skip next
2 dc, sc in next dc, **turn,** sc in each ch just completed,
slip st in next sc (sc before ch was begun), **turn,** working
behind ch-3, sc in 2 skipped dc *(Figs. 23a-d, page 123),*
★ ch 3 **loosely,** skip st where previous ch was attached and
next 2 dc, sc in next dc, **turn,** sc in each ch just completed,
slip st in next sc (sc before ch was begun), **turn,** working
behind ch-3, sc in 2 skipped dc; repeat from ★ across to
last dc, sc in last dc: 49 Cables.

Row 4: Ch 3, turn; ★ 2 dc in next sc (behind cable), dc in
next sc (behind same cable), skip sc where ch was attached
on previous row; repeat from ★ across to last sc, dc in last
sc: 149 dc.

Row 5: Ch 3, turn; dc in next dc and in each dc across;
finish off.

DIAMOND PANEL (Make 3)
Ch 151 **loosely.**

Row 1 (Right side): Dc in fourth ch from hook and in
each ch across: 149 sts.

Note: Mark last row as **right** side.

Row 2: Ch 3, turn, dc in Front Loop Only of next dc and
in each dc across *(Fig. 26, page 124).*

Row 3: Ch 3, turn; dc in both loops of next dc and in each
dc across.

Rows 4-10: Repeat Rows 2 and 3, 3 times; then repeat
Row 2 once **more.**
Finish off.

DIAMONDS
Note: Design is worked in free loops only of Diamond
Panel *(Fig. 27a, page 124).*

Row 1: With **right** side facing, join yarn with sc in third dc
on Row 1; ★ ch 11, skip next 5 dc, sc in next dc; repeat
from ★ across to last 2 dc, leave remaining sts unworked;
finish off: 24 loops.

Row 2: With **right** side facing, join yarn with sc in third dc
on Row 5; ch 5, insert hook under first loop and working
around loop, sc in sixth dc on Row 3, ★ ch 11, skip next
5 dc on Row 3, insert hook under next loop and working
around loop, sc in next dc on Row 3; repeat from ★ across,
ch 5, sc in third dc from end on Row 5; finish off.

Row 3: With **right** side facing, join yarn with sc in third dc
on Row 5; ★ ch 11, skip next 5 dc, insert hook under next
loop and working around loop, sc in next dc on Row 5;
repeat from ★ across, ch 5, sc in third dc from end on
Row 5; finish off.

Row 4: With **right** side facing, join yarn with sc in third dc
on Row 9; ch 5, insert hook under first loop and working
around loop, sc in sixth dc on Row 7, ★ ch 5, skip next
5 dc on Row 9, sc in next dc, ch 5, skip next 5 dc on
Row 7, insert hook under next loop and working around
loop, sc in next dc on Row 7; repeat from ★ across, ch 5, sc
in third dc from end on Row 9; finish off.

POPCORN PANEL (Make 2)
Ch 151 **loosely.**

Row 1: Dc in fourth ch from hook and in each ch across:
149 sts.

Note: To work **Popcorn,** 5 dc in dc indicated, drop loop
from hook, insert hook in first dc of 5-dc group, hook
dropped loop and draw through *(Fig. 9a, page 119).*

Row 2 (Right side): Ch 3, turn; dc in next 4 dc, ★ work
Popcorn in next dc, dc in next 5 dc; repeat from ★ across:
24 Popcorns.

Row 3: Ch 3, turn; dc in next dc and in each dc and each Popcorn across: 149 dc.

Row 4: Ch 3, turn; dc in next dc, work Popcorn in next dc, ★ dc in next 5 dc, work Popcorn in next dc; repeat from ★ across to last 2 dc, dc in last 2 dc: 25 Popcorns.

Row 5: Ch 3, turn; dc in next dc and in each dc and each Popcorn across: 149 dc.

Rows 6 and 7: Repeat Rows 2 and 3.

Finish off.

ASSEMBLY

With **wrong** side of Cable Panel and Diamond Panel together and working through both loops of both pieces, join yarn with sc to st at left end; working from **left** to **right**, work reverse sc in each st across *(Figs. 17a-d, page 121)*; finish off.

Join remaining Panels in same manner in the following order: Popcorn, Diamond, Popcorn, Diamond and Cable.

Add fringe *(Figs. 31b & d, page 126)*.

SPRING THROW

Delicate shells surrounded by an airy eyelet border give this mile-a-minute afghan a feeling of spring! Fashioned in shades of the early-morning sky, the simple throw is worked in easy-to-make strips using double crochet stitches and then whipstitched together.

Finished Size: Approximately 48" x 60"

MATERIALS
Worsted Weight Yarn, approximately:
  Color A (Light Peach) - 13 ounces,
    (370 grams, 855 yards)
  Color B (Peach) - 9 ounces, (260 grams, 595 yards)
  Color C (Dark Peach) - 10 ounces,
    (280 grams, 660 yards)
Crochet hook, size K (6.50 mm) **or** size needed for
  gauge
Yarn needle

GAUGE: 12 sc and 14 rows = 4"
  One Strip = 5¹/4" wide

STRIP (Make 9)
CENTER
With Color A, ch 9 **loosely.**
Row 1 (Right side): (4 Dc, ch 3, 4 dc) in sixth ch from hook, skip next 2 chs, dc in last ch: 13 sts.
Note: Loop a short piece of yarn around any stitch to mark last row as **right** side and bottom edge.
Row 2: Ch 3 **(counts as first dc, now and throughout),** turn; (4 dc, ch 3, 4 dc) in next ch-3 sp, skip next 4 dc, dc in top of beginning ch: 10 dc.
Rows 3-66: Ch 3, turn; (4 dc, ch 3, 4 dc) in next ch-3 sp, skip next 4 dc, dc in last dc.
Row 67: Ch 3, turn; slip st in next ch-3 sp, ch 3, skip next 4 dc, slip st in last dc; finish off.

BORDER
Rnd 1: With **right** side facing, join Color B with slip st in last ch-3 sp on Row 67; ch 3, (2 dc, ch 3, 3 dc) in same sp (corner); working in end of rows, 3 dc in each row across to last row, (3 dc, ch 3, 3 dc) in last row (corner); working in free loop of beginning ch *(Fig. 27b, page 124)*, dc in same ch as first (4 dc, ch 3, 4 dc); working in end of rows, (3 dc, ch 3, 3 dc) in first row (corner), 3 dc in each row across to last row, (3 dc, ch 3, 3 dc) in last row (corner); working around slip st on Row 67, dc in ch-3 sp on Row 66; join with slip st to first dc, finish off: 416 dc.
Rnd 2: With **right** side facing and working in Back Loops Only *(Fig. 26, page 124)*, join Color C with slip st in first corner ch-3 sp; ch 3, dc in same sp, † ch 1, skip next dc, (dc in next dc, ch 1, skip next dc) across to next corner ch-3 sp, (2 dc, ch 2, 2 dc) in corner sp, dc in each dc across to next corner ch-3 sp †, (2 dc, ch 2, 2 dc) in corner sp, repeat from † to † once, 2 dc in same corner sp as first dc, ch 1, hdc in first dc to form last corner ch-2 sp; do **not** finish off: 230 dc.
Rnd 3: Ch 1, 3 sc in same sp; working in Back Loops Only † sc in next dc and in each ch and each dc across to next corner ch-2 sp, 3 sc in corner sp, sc in each dc across to next corner ch-2 sp †, 3 sc in corner sp, repeat from † to † once; join with slip st to first sc, finish off.

ASSEMBLY
With **wrong** side of two Strips together, bottom edges at the same end and using Color C, whipstitch Strips together working in inside loops and beginning in center sc of first corner and ending in center sc of next corner *(Fig. 29a, page 125)*.
Join remaining Strips in same manner, always working from the same direction.

SOUTHWESTERN STRIPES

This handsome afghan will introduce a taste of the Southwest to your decor! It features shades from the Painted Desert alternated with striking tweed-look stripes that are created by holding strands of black and ecru yarn together as you crochet. The entire throw is worked in single crochet stitches, so you don't have to be an experienced hand to make it.

Finished Size: Approximately 48" x 64"

MATERIALS

Worsted Weight Yarn, approximately:
MC (Black) - 28 ounces, (800 grams, 1,775 yards)
Color A (Ecru) - 16 ounces,
(450 grams, 1,015 yards)
Color B (Light Rust) - 16 ounces,
(450 grams, 1,015 yards)
Color C (Aqua) - 8 ounces,
(230 grams, 505 yards)
Color D (Dark Aqua) - 8 ounces,
(230 grams, 505 yards)
Color E (Rust) - 8 ounces,
(230 grams, 505 yards)
Crochet hook, size K (6.50 mm) **or** size needed for gauge

Note: Entire Afghan is working holding two strands of yarn together.

GAUGE: 8 sc and 8 rows = 4"

With one strand of MC and one strand of Color A, ch 96 **loosely.**

Row 1 (Right side): Sc in second ch from hook and in each ch across: 95 sc.

Note: Loop a short piece of yarn around any stitch to mark last row as **right** side.

Rows 2-7: Ch 1, turn; sc in each sc across.

Row 8: Ch 1, turn; sc in each sc across working last sc to last step (2 loops on hook), cut Color A, complete sc with 2 strands of MC *(Fig. 28, page 124)*.

Row 9: Ch 1, turn; sc in each sc across changing to Color B in last sc.

Row 10: Ch 1, turn; sc in each sc across.

Row 11: Ch 1, turn; sc in each sc across changing to MC in last sc.

Row 12: Ch 1, turn; sc in each sc across changing to Color C in last sc.

Row 13: Ch 1, turn; sc in each sc across.

Row 14: Ch 1, turn; sc in each sc across changing to MC in last sc.

Row 15: Ch 1, turn; sc in each sc across changing to Color E in last sc.

Row 16: Ch 1, turn; sc in each sc across.

Row 17: Ch 1, turn; sc in each sc across changing to MC in last sc.

Row 18: Ch 1, turn; sc in each sc across changing to Color D in last sc.

Row 19: Ch 1, turn; sc in each sc across.

Row 20: Ch 1, turn; sc in each sc across changing to MC in last sc.

Row 21: Ch 1, turn; sc in each sc across changing to Color B in last sc.

Row 22: Ch 1, turn; sc in each sc across.

Row 23: Ch 1, turn; sc in each sc across changing to MC in last sc.

Row 24: Ch 1, turn; sc in each sc across changing to one strand of MC and one strand of Color A in last sc.

Rows 25-31: Ch 1, turn; sc in each sc across.

Rows 32-127: Repeat Rows 8-31, 4 times.

Row 128: Ch 1, turn; sc in each sc across; finish off.

21

FIELDS OF GREEN

Worked in shades of green that capture the look of a summertime meadow, this comfy ripple afghan will bring a down-home feeling to family outings. And since it's crocheted holding two strands of yarn, you'll have plenty of time for picnicking!

Finished Size: Approximately 47" x 62"

MATERIALS
Worsted Weight Yarn, approximately:
Color A (Dark Green) - 27 ounces,
(770 grams, 1,775 yards)
Color B (Green) - 24 ounces,
(680 grams, 1,580 yards)
Color C (Light Green) - 24 ounces,
(680 grams, 1,580 yards)
Crochet hook, size N (9.00 mm) **or** size needed for gauge

Note: Entire Afghan is worked holding two strands of yarn together throughout.

GAUGE: In pattern, 10 sts = 4" and 6 rows = 4¹/2"
(7³/4" point to point)

PATTERN STITCHES
DECREASE (uses next 2 sts)
★ YO, insert hook in **next** st, YO and pull up a loop, YO and draw through 2 loops on hook; repeat from ★ once **more**, YO and draw through all 3 loops on hook.

FRONT POST DOUBLE CROCHET
  (abbreviated FPdc)
YO, insert hook from **front** to **back** around post of st indicated, YO and pull up a loop even with last st worked (3 loops on hook), (YO and draw through 2 loops on hook) twice *(Fig. 11, page 119)*, skip st behind FPdc.

BEGINNING FRONT POST DECREASE
  (abbreviated beginning FP decrease) (uses next 2 sts)
YO, insert hook in **next** st, YO and pull up a loop, YO and draw through 2 loops on hook, YO, insert hook from **front** to **back** around post of **next** st, YO and pull up a loop even with last st worked, YO and draw through 2 loops on hook, YO and draw through all 3 loops on hook.

ENDING FRONT POST DECREASE
  (abbreviated ending FP decrease) (uses next 2 sts)
YO, insert hook from **front** to **back** around post of **next** st, YO and pull up a loop even with last st worked, YO and draw through 2 loops on hook, YO, insert hook in **next** st, YO and pull up a loop, YO and draw through 2 loops on hook, YO and draw through all 3 loops on hook.

STRIPE SEQUENCE
★ 4 Rows **each** of Color A, Color B, and Color C; repeat from ★ for sequence.

With Color A, ch 144 **loosely**.
Row 1 (Right side): Dc in fourth ch from hook and in each ch across: 142 sts.
Note: Loop a short piece of yarn around any stitch to mark last row as **right** side.
Row 2: Ch 3 **(counts as first dc, now and throughout)**, turn; decrease, work FPdc around next 2 dc, (dc in next 2 dc, work FPdc around next 2 dc) twice, 3 dc in next dc, work FPdc around next 2 dc, (dc in next 2 dc, work FPdc around next 2 dc) twice, ★ skip next 2 dc, work FPdc around next 2 dc, (dc in next 2 dc, work FPdc around next 2 dc) twice, 3 dc in next dc, work FPdc around next 2 dc, (dc in next 2 dc, work FPdc around next 2 dc) twice; repeat from ★ across to last 3 sts, decrease, dc in last st.
Row 3: Ch 3, turn; decrease, dc in next FPdc, (work FPdc around next 2 dc, dc in next 2 FPdc) twice, work FPdc around next dc, 3 dc in next dc, work FPdc around next dc (dc in next 2 FPdc, work FPdc around next 2 dc) twice, dc in next FPdc, ★ skip next 2 FPdc, dc in next FPdc, (work FPdc around next 2 dc, dc in next 2 FPdc) twice, work FPdc around next dc, 3 dc in next dc, work FPdc around next dc, (dc in next 2 FPdc, work FPdc around next 2 dc) twice, dc in next FPdc; repeat from ★ across to last 3 sts, decrease, dc in last dc.
Row 4: Ch 3, turn; work beginning FP decrease, dc in next 2 FPdc, (work FPdc around next 2 dc, dc in next 2 sts) twice, 3 dc in next dc, dc in next 2 sts, (work FPdc around next 2 dc, dc in next 2 FPdc) twice, ★ skip next 2 dc, dc in next 2 FPdc, (work FPdc around next 2 dc, dc in next 2 sts) twice, 3 dc in next dc, dc in next 2 sts, (work FPdc around next 2 dc, dc in next 2 FPdc) twice; repeat from ★ across to last 3 sts, work ending FP decrease, dc in last dc; finish off.

Row 5: With **right** side facing, join next color with slip st in first dc; ch 3, work beginning FP decrease, work FPdc around next dc, (dc in next 2 FPdc, work FPdc around next 2 dc) twice, dc in next dc, 3 dc in next dc, dc in next dc, (work FPdc around next 2 dc, dc in next 2 FPdc) twice, work FPdc around next dc, ★ skip next 2 dc, work FPdc around next dc, (dc in next 2 FPdc, work FPdc around next 2 dc) twice, dc in next dc, 3 dc in next dc, dc in next dc, (work FPdc around next 2 dc, dc in next 2 FPdc) twice, work FPdc around next dc; repeat from ★ across to last 3 sts, work ending FP decrease, dc in last dc.

Row 6: Ch 3, turn; decrease, work FPdc around next 2 dc, (dc in next 2 FPdc, work FPdc around next 2 dc) twice, 3 dc in next dc, work FPdc around next 2 dc, (dc in next 2 FPdc, work FPdc around next 2 dc) twice, ★ skip next 2 FPdc, work FPdc around next 2 dc, (dc in next 2 FPdc, work FPdc around next 2 dc) twice, 3 dc in next dc, work FPdc around next 2 dc, (dc in next 2 FPdc, work FPdc around next 2 dc) twice; repeat from ★ across to last 3 sts, decrease, dc in last dc.

Repeat Rows 3-6 until Afghan measures approximately 62", ending by working Row 4 with Color A.

BERRY BASKET

This luscious afghan is crocheted in the rosy shades of fresh-picked berries. Worked in strips of double and single crochet stitches with front post stitches, the mile-a-minute throw is a perfect breakfast companion for a cool country morning.

Finished Size: Approximately 54" x 72"

MATERIALS
Worsted Weight Yarn, approximately:
  MC (Light Rose) - 37¹/2 ounces,
    (1,070 grams, 2,465 yards)
  CC (Rose) - 19¹/2 ounces, (550 grams, 1,280 yards)
  Crochet hook, size G (4.00 mm) **or** size needed for gauge
  Yarn needle

GAUGE: 16 dc and 8 rows = 4"
    One Strip = 4¹/2" wide

STRIP (Make 12)
With MC, ch 279 **loosely**.
Foundation Row (Right side)**:** Dc in fourth ch from hook and in each ch across; finish off: 277 sts.
Note: Loop a short piece of yarn around last dc made to mark last row as **right** side and bottom edge.

FIRST SIDE
Row 1: With **right** side facing, join MC with slip st in top of beginning ch; ch 3 **(counts as first dc, now and throughout)**, ★ skip next 2 dc, 5 dc in next dc, skip next 2 dc, dc in next dc; repeat from ★ across; finish off: 277 dc.
Row 2: With **right** side facing, join CC with slip st in first dc; ch 3, skip next 2 dc, 3 dc in next dc, ★ skip next 2 dc, work 3 FPdc around next dc *(Fig. 11, page 119)*, skip dc behind FPdc and next 2 dc, 3 dc in next dc; repeat from ★ across to last 3 dc, skip next 2 dc, dc in last dc; finish off: 135 FPdc.
Row 3: With **right** side facing, join MC with slip st in first dc; ch 3, ★ dc in next 3 dc, work FPtr around next 3 FPdc *(Fig. 12, page 119)*, skip FPdc behind each FPtr; repeat from ★ across to last 4 dc, dc in last 4 dc; finish off: 275 sts.

Row 4: With **right** side facing and working in Back Loops Only *(Fig. 26, page 124)*, join CC with slip st in first dc; ch 1, sc in same st and in each st across; finish off.

SECOND SIDE
Row 1: With **right** side facing and working in free loops of beginning ch *(Fig. 27b, page 124)*, join MC with slip st in first ch; ch 3, ★ skip next 2 chs, 5 dc in next ch, skip next 2 chs, dc in next ch; repeat from ★ 45 times **more**; finish off: 277 dc.
Rows 2-4: Work same as First Side.

ASSEMBLY
With **wrong** side of two Strips together, bottom edges at the same end and using CC, whipstitch Strips together working in inside loops *(Fig. 29a, page 125)*.
Join remaining Strips in same manner, always working from the same direction.

EDGING
With **right** side of short end facing and working in end of rows, join CC with slip st in first row; ch 2, 2 dc in each of next 2 rows, 2 tr in next row, 3 tr in next row (Foundation Row), 2 tr in next row, 2 dc in each of next 2 rows, hdc in next row, ★ skip joining, hdc in next row, 2 dc in each of next 2 rows, 2 tr in next row, 3 tr in next row (Foundation Row), 2 tr in next row, 2 dc in each of next 2 rows, hdc in next row; repeat from ★ across; finish off.
Repeat across opposite end.

COZY WRAP

Old-fashioned styling makes this cozy wrap look right at home with your antique collectibles! Crocheted holding three strands of yarn together and using a jumbo hook, the throw features square motifs worked in rounds of double crochet stitches. A picot edging adds a charming finishing touch.

Finished Size: Approximately 48" x 66"

MATERIALS
Worsted Weight Yarn, approximately:
59 ounces, (1,680 grams, 3,710 yards)
Crochet hook, size Q (15.00 mm) **or** size needed for gauge

Note: Entire Afghan is worked holding 3 strands of yarn together.

GAUGE: One Motif = 8"

MOTIF (Make 35)
Rnd 1 (Right side): Leaving a 3" end, wrap yarn around finger once to form a ring, insert hook in ring, YO and pull up a loop *(Fig. 25, page 124)*, ch 4 **(counts as first dc plus ch 1, now and throughout)**, (3 dc in ring, ch 1) 3 times, 2 dc in ring; join with slip st to first dc, pull yarn end to close ring: 16 sts.
Note: Loop a short piece of yarn around any stitch to mark last round as **right** side.
Rnd 2: (Slip st, ch 4, dc) in first ch-1 sp, dc in next 3 dc, ★ (dc, ch 1, dc) in next ch-1 sp, dc in next 3 dc; repeat from ★ around; join with slip st to first dc: 24 sts.
Rnd 3: (Slip st, ch 3, dc, ch 1, 2 dc) in first ch-1 sp, dc in next 5 dc, ★ (2 dc, ch 1, 2 dc) in next ch-1 sp, dc in next 5 dc; repeat from ★ around; join with slip st to top of beginning ch-3, finish off: 40 sts.

ASSEMBLY
Afghan is assembled by joining Motifs together, forming 5 vertical strips of 7 Motifs each and then by joining strips. Join Motifs as follows: With **wrong** sides together and working through inside loops, join yarn with slip st in corner ch-1 sp; ch 1, (slip st in next dc, ch 1) across, slip st in next corner ch-1 sp; finish off.
Join strips in same manner, being sure to slip st in joinings between Motifs to avoid holes.

EDGING
Rnd 1: With **right** side of long edge facing, join yarn with slip st in corner ch-1 sp; ch 1, ★ 3 sc in corner sp, working in Back Loops Only *(Fig. 26, page 124)*, sc in next 9 dc, (sc in next 2 ch-1 sps, sc in next 9 dc) across to next corner ch-1 sp, 3 sc in corner sp, 2 sc in next dc, sc in next 8 dc, (sc in next 2 ch-1 sps, sc in next 9 dc) across to next corner ch-1 sp; repeat from ★ around; join with slip st to **both** loops of first sc: 270 sc.
Rnd 2: Working in both loops, slip st in next sc, ch 7, dc in fourth ch from hook, dc in same sc, skip next 2 sc, ★ dc in next sc, ch 4, dc in fourth ch from hook, dc in same sc, skip next 2 sc; repeat from ★ around; join with slip st to third ch of beginning ch-7, finish off.

COUNTRY LANE

Crocheted in shades of dusty brown, this mile-a-minute throw brings to mind images of leisurely strolls down quiet country lanes. The afghan works up in a jiffy because you use basic single and double crochet stitches, and only three additional rounds are added to the foundation row of each strip.

Finished Size: Approximately 54" x 72"

MATERIALS
Worsted Weight Yarn, approximately:
  MC (Brown) - 29 ounces, (820 grams, 1,905 yards)
  CC (Light Brown) - 16 ounces,
    (450 grams, 1,050 yards)
Crochet hook, size K (6.50 mm) **or** size needed for gauge
Yarn needle

GAUGE: 12 dc and 8 rows = 4"
      One Strip = 3" wide

STRIP (Make 18)
With MC, ch 213 **loosely**.
Foundation Row (Right side): Dc in fourth ch from hook and in each ch across; finish off: 211 sts.
Note: Loop a short piece of yarn around last dc made to mark last row as **right** side and bottom edge.

EDGING
Rnd 1: With **right** side facing, join CC with slip st in top of beginning ch; ch 1, sc in same st, (ch 3, skip next dc, sc in next dc) across, ch 4; working in free loops of beginning ch (**Fig. 27b, page 124**), sc in first ch, (ch 3, skip next ch, sc in next ch) 105 times, ch 1, dc in first sc to form last ch-4 sp: 212 sps.
Rnd 2: Ch 1, (sc, ch 3) twice in same sp, sc in next ch-3 sp, ch 3, place marker around last ch-3 made to mark Border placement, (sc in next ch-3 sp, ch 3) 104 times, (sc, ch 3) twice in next ch-4 sp, (sc in next ch-3 sp, ch 3) around; join with slip st to first sc, finish off: 214 ch-3 sps.

BORDER
With **right** side facing, join MC with slip st in marked ch-3 sp; ch 3 (**counts as first dc**), 2 dc in same sp, † (2 dc in next ch-3 sp, 3 dc in next ch-3 sp) 52 times, 5 dc in next ch-3 sp †, 3 dc in each of next 2 ch-3 sps, repeat from † to † once, 3 dc in last ch-3 sp; join with slip st to first dc, finish off: 542 dc.

ASSEMBLY
With **wrong** side of two Strips together, bottom edges at the same end and using MC, whipstitch Strips together working in inside loops across length of Strip (**Fig. 29a, page 125**).
Join remaining Strips in same manner, always working from the same direction.

COBBLESTONES

Crocheted in a warm neutral, this mile-a-minute throw will add a cozy touch to your country decor. The uniquely textured strips feature tiny "cobblestones" created with double treble and single crochet stitches.

Finished Size: Approximately 47" x 62"

MATERIALS
Worsted Weight Yarn, approximately:
    44 ounces, (1,250 grams, 2,890 yards)
Crochet hook, size K (6.50 mm) **or** size needed for
    gauge
Yarn needle

GAUGE: 12 sc and 14 rows = 4"
           One Strip = 4³/4" wide

STRIP (Make 10)
CENTER
Ch 6 **loosely.**

Row 1: Sc in second ch from hook and in each ch across: 5 sc.

Row 2 (Right side): Ch 3 **(counts as first dc, now and throughout)**, turn; dc in next sc and in each sc across.

Note: Loop a short piece of yarn around any stitch to mark last row as **right** side and bottom edge.

Row 3: Ch 3, turn; dc in next dc and in each dc across.

Row 4: Ch 1, turn; sc in first dc, skip next 2 dc, work FPtr around next dc **(Fig. 12, page 119)**, working **behind** FPtr just made, sc in second skipped dc, working in **front** of FPtr, work FPtr around first skipped dc, skip next dc, sc in last dc: 5 sts.

Row 5: Ch 3, turn; dc in next st and in each st across.

Row 6: Ch 1, turn; sc in first dc, skip first FPtr one row **below**, work FPtr around next FPtr one row **below**, skip dc **behind** FPtr just made, sc in next dc, working in **front** of FPtr, work FPtr around skipped FPtr, skip dc behind FPtr, sc in last dc: 5 sts.

Rows 7-109: Repeat Rows 5 and 6, 51 times; then repeat Row 5 once **more.**

Row 110: Ch 1, turn; sc in each dc across; do **not** finish off.

BORDER
Rnd 1: Ch 1, do **not** turn; working in end of rows, sc in first row, (2 sc in next row, sc in next row) across to last 3 rows, 2 sc in each of next 2 rows, sc in last row; working in free loops of beginning ch **(Fig. 27b, page 124)**, sc in first ch, skip next ch, 7 tr in next ch, place marker around last tr made, skip next ch, sc in next ch; working in end of rows, sc in first row, 2 sc in each of next 2 rows, sc in next row, (2 sc in next row, sc in next row) across; working across sts on Row 110, sc in first sc, skip next sc, 7 tr in next sc, skip next sc, sc in last sc; join with slip st to first sc: 348 sts.

Rnd 2: Ch 1, turn; sc in first sc, dtr in next tr **(Figs. 8a & b, page 118)**, (sc in next tr, dtr in next tr) 3 times, place marker around last dtr made, sc in next sc, (dtr in next sc, sc in next sc) across to next marker, dtr in marked tr, remove marker, (sc in next tr, dtr in next tr) 3 times, place marker around last dtr made, (sc in next sc, dtr in next sc) around; join with slip st to first sc.

Note: To work **V-St**, (dc, ch 1, dc) in next sc.

Rnd 3: Ch 4, turn; dc in same st, skip next dtr, work V-St, (skip next dtr, work V-St) across to next marker, ch 1, skip marked dtr, remove marker, place marker around ch-1 just made, work V-St, (ch 1, skip next dtr, work V-St) 3 times, (skip next dtr, work V-St) across to next marker, ch 1, skip marked dtr, remove marker, place marker around ch-1 just made, (work V-St, ch 1, skip next dtr) 3 times; join with slip st to third ch of beginning ch-4.

Rnd 4: Do **not** turn; slip st in first ch-1 sp, ch 1, sc in same sp, † (skip next dc, sc in sp **before** next dc and in next ch-1 sp) across to next marker, sc in marked ch-1 sp, remove marker, place marker around sc just made for joining placement, sc in same sp, 2 sc in each of next 6 ch-1 sps, place marker around last sc made for joining placement †, sc in next ch-1 sp, repeat from † to † once; join with slip st to first sc, finish off.

ASSEMBLY
With **wrong** side of two Strips together and bottom edges at the same end, whipstitch Strips together working in inside loops and working from marked stitch to marked stitch across long edge **(Fig. 29a, page 125)**.

Join remaining Strips in same manner, always working from the same direction.

BLUE AND WHITE FAVORITE

Reminiscent of Grandmother's blue and white china, this country throw will become a family favorite! The hexagon motifs, created with double crochet stitches and accented with front post stitches, work up fast holding double strands of yarn.

Finished Size: Approximately 47" x 63"

MATERIALS
Worsted Weight Yarn, approximately:
MC (White) - 33 ounces, (940 grams, 1,925 yards)
Color A (Light Blue) - 17 ounces,
(480 grams, 990 yards)
Color B (Blue) - 11 ounces, (310 grams, 640 yards)
Crochet hook, size N (9.00 mm) **or** size needed for gauge
Yarn needle

Note: Entire Afghan is worked holding two strands of yarn together.

GAUGE: One Motif = 10¹/2"
(from straight edge to straight edge)

MOTIF (Make 27)

With Color B, ch 5; join with slip st to form a ring.
Rnd 1 (Right side)**:** Ch 3 **(counts as first dc, now and throughout)**, 2 dc in ring, ch 1, (3 dc in ring, ch 1) 5 times; join with slip st to first dc: 18 dc.
Note: Loop a short piece of yarn around any stitch to mark last round as **right** side.
Rnd 2: Ch 3, dc in same st and in next dc, 2 dc in next dc, ch 1, ★ 2 dc in next dc, dc in next dc, 2 dc in next dc, ch 1; repeat from ★ around; join with slip st to first dc, finish off: 30 dc.
Rnd 3: With **right** side facing, join Color A with slip st in same st as joining; ch 3, dc in same st and in next dc, work FPdtr around next dc *(Fig. 13, page 120)*, skip dc behind FPdtr, dc in next dc, 2 dc in next dc, ch 1, ★ 2 dc in next dc, dc in next dc, work FPdtr around next dc, skip dc behind FPdtr, dc in next dc, 2 dc in next dc, ch 1; repeat from ★ around; join with slip st to first dc: 6 FPdtr.
Rnd 4: Ch 3, dc in same st and in next 5 sts, 2 dc in next dc, ch 1, ★ 2 dc in next dc, dc in next 5 sts, 2 dc in next dc, ch 1; repeat from ★ around; join with slip st to first dc, finish off: 54 dc.
Rnd 5: With **right** side facing, join MC with slip st in same st as joining; ch 3, dc in same st and in next dc, work FPdtr around next dc, skip dc behind FPdtr, dc in next 3 dc, work FPdtr around next dc, skip dc behind FPdtr, dc in next dc, 2 dc in next dc, ch 1, ★ 2 dc in next dc, dc in next dc, work FPdtr around next dc, skip dc behind FPdtr, dc in next 3 dc, work FPdtr around next dc, skip dc behind FPdtr, dc in next dc, 2 dc in next dc, ch 1; repeat from ★ around; join with slip st to first dc: 12 FPdtr.
Rnd 6: Ch 3, dc in same st and in next 9 sts, 2 dc in next dc, ch 1, ★ 2 dc in next dc, dc in next 9 sts, 2 dc in next dc, ch 1; repeat from ★ around; join with slip st to first dc, finish off: 78 dc.

ASSEMBLY

With **wrong** sides together, using MC and working through inside loops, whipstitch Motifs together, forming 3 vertical strips of 5 Motifs each and 2 vertical strips of 6 Motifs each *(Fig. 29a, page 125)*; and then whipstitch strips together alternating strips of 5-6-5-6-5 Motifs.

PEACHES & CREAM

You can enjoy the orchard-fresh goodness of summer peaches with this easy-to-make afghan! The mile-a-minute strips feature creamy shells surrounded by V-stitch borders in peach and leafy green.

Finished Size: Approximately 49" x 63"

MATERIALS
Worsted Weight Yarn, approximately:
Color A (Off-White) - 20 ounces,
(570 grams, 1,315 yards)
Color B (Tan) - 7 ounces, (200 grams, 460 yards)
Color C (Peach) - 7 ounces,
(200 grams, 460 yards)
Color D (Green) - 8 ounces,
(230 grams, 525 yards)
Crochet hook, size K (6.50 mm) **or** size needed for gauge

GAUGE: 12 sc and 14 rows = 4"
One Strip = 7" wide

STRIP (Make 7)
CENTER
With Color A, ch 14 **loosely**.
Row 1 (Right side): Sc in second ch from hook and in each ch across: 13 sc.
Note #1: Loop a short piece of yarn around any stitch to mark last row as **right** side and bottom edge.
Note #2: To work **Shell**, (2 dc, ch 1, 2 dc) in st or sp indicated.
Row 2: Ch 3 **(counts as first dc, now and throughout)**, turn; ★ skip next 2 sc, work Shell in next sc, skip next 2 sc, dc in next sc; repeat from ★ once **more**: 11 dc.
Rows 3-88: Ch 3, turn; ★ work Shell in next ch-1 sp, skip next 2 dc, dc in next dc; repeat from ★ once **more**.
Row 89: Ch 1, turn; sc in each dc and in each ch across; finish off: 13 sc.

BORDER
Note: To work **V-St**, (dc, ch 1, dc) in st or sp indicated.
Rnd 1: With **right** side facing and working in end of rows, join Color B with slip st in Row 89; ch 4 **(counts as first dc plus ch 1, now and throughout)**, (dc, ch 2, work V-St) in same row (corner), work V-St in each row across to last row, work (V-St, ch 2, V-St) in last row (corner); working in free loops of beginning ch **(Fig. 27b, page 124)**, skip first 3 chs, work V-St in next ch, (skip next 2 chs, work V-St in next ch) twice, skip next 3 chs; working in end of rows, work (V-St, ch 2, V-St) in first row (corner), work V-St in each row across to last row, work (V-St, ch 2, V-St) in last row (corner); working across sts on Row 89, skip first 3 sc, work V-St in next sc, (skip next 2 sc, work V-St in next sc) twice, skip last 3 sc; join with slip st to first dc, finish off: 188 V-Sts.
Rnd 2: With **right** side facing, join Color C with slip st in first corner ch-2 sp; ch 4, (dc, ch 2, work V-St) in same sp, work V-St in each ch-1 sp across to next corner ch-2 sp, ★ work (V-St, ch 2, V-St) in corner sp, work V-St in each ch-1 sp across to next corner ch-2 sp; repeat from ★ around; join with slip st to first dc, finish off: 196 V-Sts.
Rnd 3: With **right** side facing, join Color D with slip st in first corner ch-2 sp; ch 4, (dc, ch 2, work V-St) in same sp, work V-St in each ch-1 sp across to next corner ch-2 sp, ★ work (V-St, ch 2, V-St) in corner sp, work V-St in each ch-1 sp across to next corner ch-2 sp; repeat from ★ around; join with slip st to first dc, finish off: 204 V-Sts.
Rnd 4: With **right** side facing, join Color A with slip st in first corner ch-2 sp; ch 1, (sc, ch 1, sc) in same sp and in each ch-1 sp around; join with slip st to first sc, finish off.

ASSEMBLY
With **wrong** side of two Strips together, bottom edges at the same end and working through both thicknesses, join Color A with slip st in corner ch-1 sp; (ch 1, sc) in same sp and in each ch-1 sp across to next corner ch-1 sp; finish off. Join remaining Strips in same manner, always working from the same direction.

PLUSH POLKA DOTS

Accented with popcorn stitch "polka dots," this ripple afghan features unusual textured seams created with front and back post treble crochet stitches. The wrap is quick to finish because you work it in a loose gauge using a large hook and two strands of yarn held together.

Finished Size: Approximately 52" x 70"

MATERIALS
Worsted Weight Yarn, approximately:
72 ounces, (2,040 grams, 4,735 yards)
Crochet hook, size N (9.00 mm) **or** size needed for gauge

Note: Entire Afghan is worked holding two strands of yarn together.

GAUGE: In pattern, 8 dc and 4 rows = 3¹/₂"
(8³/₄ point to point)

PATTERN STITCHES
BACK POST TREBLE CROCHET
(*abbreviated BPtr*)
YO twice, insert hook from **back** to **front** around post of st indicated, YO and pull up a loop (4 loops on hook) (*Fig. 14, page 120*), (YO and draw through 2 loops on hook) 3 times.

FRONT POST TREBLE CROCHET
(*abbreviated FPtr*)
YO twice, insert hook from **front** to **back** around post of st indicated, YO and pull up a loop (4 loops on hook) (*Fig. 12, page 119*), (YO and draw through 2 loops on hook) 3 times.

POPCORN
5 Dc in next dc, drop loop from hook, insert hook in first dc of 5-dc group, hook dropped loop and draw through (*Fig. 9a, page 119*).

Ch 138 **loosely.**

Row 1 (Right side)**:** Dc in fourth ch from hook and in next 8 chs, 3 dc in next ch, dc in next 10 chs, ★ skip next 2 chs, dc in next 10 chs, 3 dc in next ch, dc in next 10 chs; repeat from ★ across: 138 sts.

Note #1: Loop a short piece of yarn around any stitch to mark last row as **right** side.

Note #2: Work in Back Loops Only throughout (*Fig. 26, page 124*).

Row 2: Ch 3 (**counts as first dc, now and throughout**), turn; skip next dc, dc in next 10 dc, work BPtr around same st as last dc worked, dc in same st, ★ dc in next 10 dc, skip next 2 dc, dc in next 11 dc, work BPtr around same st as last dc worked, dc in same st; repeat from ★ across to last 11 sts, dc in next 9 dc, skip next dc, dc in last st.

Row 3: Ch 3, turn; skip next dc, dc in next 4 dc, work Popcorn, dc in next 4 dc and in next BPtr, work FPtr around same st as last dc worked, dc in same st, ★ dc in next 4 dc, work Popcorn, dc in next 5 dc, skip next 2 dc, dc in next 5 dc, work Popcorn, dc in next 4 dc and in next BPtr, work FPtr around same st as last dc worked, dc in same st; repeat from ★ across to last 11 dc, dc in next 4 dc, work Popcorn, dc in next 4 dc, skip next dc, dc in last dc: 12 Popcorns.

Row 4: Ch 3, turn; skip next dc, dc in next 9 sts and in next FPtr, work BPtr around same st as last dc worked, dc in same st, ★ dc in next 10 sts, skip next 2 dc, dc in next 10 sts and in next FPtr, work BPtr around same st as last dc worked, dc in same st; repeat from ★ across to last 11 sts, dc in next 9 sts, skip next dc, dc in last dc: 138 sts.

Row 5: Ch 3, turn; skip next dc, dc in next 9 dc and in next BPtr, work FPtr around same st as last dc worked, dc in same st, ★ dc in next 10 dc, skip next 2 dc, dc in next 10 dc and in next BPtr, work FPtr around same st as last dc worked, dc in same st; repeat from ★ across to last 11 sts, dc in next 9 dc, skip next dc, dc in last dc.

Row 6: Ch 3, turn; skip next dc, dc in next 9 dc and in next FPtr, work BPtr around same st as last dc worked, dc in same st, ★ dc in next 10 dc, skip next 2 dc, dc in next 10 dc and in next FPtr, work BPtr around same st as last dc worked, dc in same st; repeat from ★ across to last 11 dc, dc in next 9 dc, skip next dc, dc in last dc.

Repeat Rows 3-6 until Afghan measures approximately 70", ending by working Row 5.
Finish off.

COLORFUL MIX

From sunny motifs to simple stripes, these fun afghans are alive with vibrant hues. Crayon-inspired patterns or bold checkerboard blocks will be a hit with youngsters, and a throw worked in varsity colors will suit the team champ. You can also paint a vivid seascape or deck the halls with holiday cheer. Whatever the occasion, these quick-to-crochet comforters make it easy to wrap your home in fabulous color!

PAINTED DESERT

*Shades of the Southwest paint this tier-drop afghan with rustic beauty.
Crocheted in stripes using a large hook, the handsome pattern brings to mind
images of warm desert sunsets. It's the perfect accent for your Western decor!*

Finished Size: Approximately 48" x 65"

MATERIALS
Worsted Weight Yarn, approximately;
    Assorted colors - 40 ounces,
        (1,140 grams, 2,630 yards) **total**
    Note: 2 Rows in pattern require approximately
        35 yards.
Crochet hook, size K (6.50 mm) **or** size needed for
gauge

GAUGE: In pattern, 12 sts and 8 rows = 4"

Note: Change colors every 2 rows as desired (**Fig. 28,
page 124**).

With first color, ch 145 **loosely**.
Row 1 (Right side)**:** Dc in fourth ch from hook and in
next ch (**3 skipped chs count as first dc**), ★ ch 1, skip
next ch, dc in next 3 chs; repeat from ★ across:
36 3-dc groups.
Note: Loop a short piece of yarn around any stitch to mark
last row as **right** side.
Row 2: Ch 3 (**counts as first dc, now and throughout**),
turn; dc in next 2 dc, (ch 1, dc in next 3 dc) across.
Note: To work **Long double crochet (abbreviated LDC),**
YO, insert hook in next ch-1 sp 2 rows **below**, YO and pull
up a loop even with hook, (YO and draw through 2 loops
on hook) twice (**Fig. 19, page 122**).
Row 3: Ch 4 (**counts as first dc plus ch 1, now and
throughout**), turn; skip next dc, dc in next dc, ★ work
LDC, dc in next dc, ch 1, skip next dc, dc in next dc;
repeat from ★ across: 35 LDC.
Row 4: Ch 4, turn; skip first ch-1, ★ dc in next 3 sts, ch 1,
skip next ch-1; repeat from ★ across to last dc, dc in last
dc: 35 3-dc groups.
Row 5: Ch 3, turn; work LDC, dc in next dc, ★ ch 1, skip
next dc, dc in next dc, work LDC, dc in next dc; repeat
from ★ across: 36 LDC.
Row 6: Ch 3, turn; dc in next 2 sts, ★ ch 1, skip next
ch-1, dc in next 3 sts; repeat from ★ across: 36 3-dc groups.
Repeat Rows 3-6 until Afghan measures approximately 65",
ending by working a **wrong** side row.
Finish off.

Add fringe in each ch-1 sp across (**Figs. 31a & c,
page 126**).

BOLD BEAUTY

Bold red and black yarns give this afghan its dramatic beauty. The "X" on each square takes on a sculptured look when you add the second color. Extra cozy and quick to finish, the wrap is crocheted using a jumbo hook and two strands of yarn held together.

Finished Size: Approximately 53" x 68"

MATERIALS
Worsted Weight Yarn, approximately:
Color A (Red) - 46 ounces,
(1,310 grams, 3,155 yards)
Color B (Black) - 36 ounces,
(1,020 grams, 2,470 yards)
Crochet hook, size P (10.00 mm) **or** size needed for gauge

Note: Entire Afghan is worked holding two strands of yarn together.

GAUGE: One Square = 7^1/2"

PATTERN STITCHES
FRONT POST DOUBLE CROCHET
(abbreviated FPdc)
YO, insert hook from **front** to **back** around post of st indicated, YO and pull up a loop (3 loops on hook), (YO and draw through 2 loops on hook) twice *(Fig. 11, page 119)*.

FRONT POST TREBLE CROCHET
(abbreviated FPtr)
YO twice, insert hook from **front** to **back** around post of st indicated, YO and pull up a loop (4 loops on hook), (YO and draw through 2 loops on hook) 3 times *(Fig. 12, page 119)*.

FRONT POST DOUBLE TREBLE CROCHET
(abbreviated FPdtr)
YO 3 times, insert hook from **front** to **back** around post of st indicated, YO and pull up a loop (5 loops on hook), (YO and draw through 2 loops on hook) 4 times *(Fig. 13, page 120)*.

SQUARE #1 (Make 31)
With Color A, ch 4; join with slip st to form a ring.
Rnd 1 (Right side): Ch 2 **(counts as first hdc)**, 2 hdc in ring, ch 1, (3 hdc in ring, ch 1) 3 times; join with slip st to first hdc: 12 hdc.
Note: Loop a short piece of yarn around any stitch to mark last round as **right** side.

Rnd 2: Ch 1, sc in same st and in next 2 hdc, 3 sc in next ch-1 sp (corner), ★ sc in next 3 hdc, 3 sc in next ch-1 sp (corner); repeat from ★ around; join with slip st to first sc: 24 sc.
Rnd 3: Ch 1, sc in same st and in each sc across to next corner sc, 3 sc in corner, (sc in each sc across to next corner sc, 3 sc in corner) 3 times, sc in last sc; join with slip st to first sc: 32 sc.
Rnd 4: Ch 1, sc in same st and in each sc across to next corner sc, 3 sc in corner, (sc in each sc across to next corner sc, 3 sc in corner) 3 times, sc in last 2 sc; join with slip st to first sc, finish off: 40 sc.
Rnd 5: With **right** side facing, skip any corner sc and join Color B with slip st in next sc; ch 1, sc in same st and in next sc, work FPdc around sc in rnd **below** next sc, work FPtr around sc 2 rnds **below** next sc, work 2 FPdtr around hdc 3 rnds **below** next sc, work FPtr around sc 2 rnds **below** next sc, work FPdc around sc in rnd **below** next sc, skip 5 sc behind post sts, sc in next 2 sc, 3 sc in next corner sc, ★ sc in next 2 sc, work FPdc around sc in rnd **below** next sc, work FPtr around sc 2 rnds **below** next sc, work 2 FPdtr around hdc 3 rnds **below** next sc, work FPtr around sc 2 rnds **below** next sc, work FPdc around sc in rnd **below** next sc, skip 5 sc behind post sts, sc in next 2 sc, 3 sc in next corner sc; repeat from ★ around; join with slip st to first sc.
Rnd 6: Ch 1, sc in same st and in next 2 sts, working through **both** loops of sts on Rnd 5 **and** through Back Loops Only of skipped sts on Rnd 4 *(Fig. 26, page 124)*, sc in next 5 sts, sc in next 3 sts, 3 sc in next corner sc, ★ sc in next 4 sts, working through **both** loops on sts on Rnd 5 **and** through Back Loops Only of skipped sts on Rnd 4, sc in next 5 sts, sc in next 3 sts, 3 sc in next corner sc; repeat from ★ around to last st, sc in last st; join with slip st to first sc, finish off.

SQUARE #2 (Make 32)
With Color B, work same as Square #1 through Rnd 4.
Rnds 5 and 6: With Color A, work same as Square #1.

ASSEMBLY
Afghan is assembled by joining Squares together, forming 7 vertical strips of 9 Squares each and then by joining strips.

Join Squares alternating Square #1 and Square #2, forming 4 strips with Square #2 as first and last Square of each strip and forming 3 strips with Square #1 as first and last Square of each strip.

Join Squares as follows: With **right** side of Square #1 and Square #2 together and working through outside loops, join Color B with slip st in corner sc; slip st in each sc across to next corner sc; finish off.

Join strips in same manner.

EDGING

With **right** side facing and working in Back Loops Only, join Color B with slip st in any corner sc; ch 1, sc in each sc around working 3 sc in each corner sc; join with slip st to first sc, finish off.

COLOR IT EASY

Alive with color, this easy-to-make throw features brilliant textured stripes created with easy double crochet and slip stitches. The multicolored wrap is worked with a large hook while holding two strands of yarn together, so you can complete it in no time!

Finished Size: Approximately 45" x 60"

MATERIALS
Worsted Weight Yarn, approximately:
   MC (Violet) - 21 ounces,
      (600 grams, 1,380 yards)
   Color A (Fuschia) - 19 ounces,
      (540 grams, 1,250 yards)
   Color B (Iris) - 16 ounces,
      (450 grams, 1,050 yards)
   Crochet hook, size N (9.00 mm) **or** size needed for
      gauge

Note: Entire Afghan is worked holding two strands of
   yarn together.

GAUGE: 10 dc and 6 rows = 4"

STRIPE SEQUENCE
One row MC, ★ one row Color A, one row Color B, one row MC; repeat from ★ throughout.

With MC, ch 107 **loosely**.
Row 1 (Right side): Dc in fourth ch from hook and in each ch across changing to Color A in last dc *(Fig. 28, page 124)*: 105 sts.
Note: Loop a short piece of yarn around any stitch to mark last row as **right** side.
Row 2: Ch 1, turn; slip st in first st, (dc in next st, slip st in next st) across changing to next color in last slip st.
Row 3: Ch 3 **(counts as first dc, now and throughout)**, turn; dc in next dc and in each st across changing to next color in last dc: 105 dc.
Repeat Rows 2 and 3 until Afghan measures approximately 57", ending by working Row 3 with MC; do **not** finish off.
First Side: Ch 1, sc evenly across end of rows; finish off.
Second Side: With **right** side facing, join MC with slip st in end of first row; ch 1, sc evenly across end of rows; finish off.

EDGING
Rnd 1: With **right** side facing, join Color A with slip st in any corner st; ch 3, dc in each st around working 3 dc in each corner st; join with slip st to first dc, finish off.
Rnd 2: With **right** side facing and working in horizontal strand of each dc *(Fig. 20, page 122)*, join MC with slip st in any corner dc; ch 3, dc in each dc around working 3 dc in each corner dc; join with slip st to first dc, finish off.

SHADES OF THE SEA

Reminiscent of frothy ocean waves, these ripples of aqua and cream show off a treasure trove of delicate shells. Easy-to-make tassels add flair to the throw, which is worked using double strands of yarn.

Finished Size: Approximately 48" x 63"

MATERIALS
Worsted Weight Yarn, approximately:
Color A (Aqua) - 22^1/$_2$ ounces,
(640 grams, 1,480 yards)
Color B (Ecru) - 19 ounces,
(540 grams, 1,250 yards)
Color C (Light Aqua) - 22^1/$_2$ ounces,
(640 grams, 1,480 yards)
Crochet hook, size K (6.50 mm) **or** size needed for gauge

Note: Entire Afghan is worked holding two strands of yarn together.

GAUGE: 9 sts (point to point) and 8 rows = 4^3/$_4$"

PATTERN STITCHES
SHELL
(2 Dc, ch 3, 2 dc) in ch-3 sp one row **below** ch-4.
DECREASE (uses next 3 sc)
YO, insert hook in **next** sc, YO and pull up a loop, YO and draw through 2 loops on hook, YO, skip **next** sc, insert hook in **next** sc, YO and pull up a loop, YO and draw through 2 loops on hook, YO and draw through all 3 loops on hook.

With Color A, ch 164 **loosely**.
Row 1 (Right side): Dc in fifth ch from hook, ch 1, (skip next ch, dc in next ch, ch 1) twice, YO, skip next ch, insert hook in next ch, YO and pull up a loop, YO and draw through 2 loops on hook, YO, skip next 2 chs, insert hook in next ch, YO and pull up a loop, YO and draw through 2 loops on hook, YO and draw through all 3 loops on hook, ch 1, (skip next ch, dc in next ch, ch 1) twice, ★ skip next ch, 2 dc in next ch, ch 3, 2 dc in next ch, ch 1, (skip next ch, dc in next ch, ch 1) twice, YO, skip next ch, insert hook in next ch, YO and pull up a loop, YO and draw through 2 loops on hook, YO, skip next 2 chs, insert hook in next ch, YO and pull up a loop, YO and draw through 2 loops on hook, YO and draw through all 3 loops on hook, ch 1, (skip next ch, dc in next ch, ch 1) twice; repeat from ★ across to last 2 chs, skip next ch, (dc, ch 1, dc) in last ch changing to Color B in last dc **(Fig. 28, page 124):** 90 sts.

Note: Loop a short piece of yarn around any stitch to mark last row as **right** side.
Row 2: Ch 1, turn; sc in first dc, (ch 1, sc in next dc) 3 times, skip next ch-1 sp, sc in next st and in next dc, (ch 1, sc in next dc) twice, ★ ch 4, skip next 2 dc, sc in next dc, (ch 1, sc in next dc) twice, skip next ch-1 sp, sc in next st and in next dc, (ch 1, sc in next dc) twice; repeat from ★ 8 times **more**, ch 1, skip next ch, sc in next ch changing to Color C.
Row 3: Ch 4 (**counts as first dc plus ch 1, now and throughout**), turn; dc in same st, ch 1, (dc in next sc, ch 1) twice, decrease, ch 1, (dc in next sc, ch 1) twice, ★ holding next ch-4 in **back**, work Shell, ch 1, (dc in next sc, ch 1) twice, decrease, ch 1, (dc in next sc, ch 1) twice; repeat from ★ across to last sc, (dc, ch 1, dc) in last sc changing to Color B in last dc.
Row 4: Ch 1, turn; sc in first dc, (ch 1, sc in next dc) 3 times, skip next ch-1 sp, sc in next st and in next dc, (ch 1, sc in next dc) twice, ★ ch 4, skip next 2 dc, sc in next dc, (ch 1, sc in next dc) twice, skip next ch-1 sp, sc in next st and in next dc, (ch 1, sc in next dc) twice; repeat from ★ 8 times **more**, ch 1, skip next ch, sc in next ch changing to Color A in last sc.
Row 5: Ch 4, turn; dc in same st, ch 1, (dc in next sc, ch 1) twice, decrease, ch 1, (dc in next sc, ch 1) twice, ★ holding next ch-4 in **back**, work Shell, ch 1, (dc in next sc, ch 1) twice, decrease, ch 1, (dc in next sc, ch 1) twice; repeat from ★ across to last sc, (dc, ch 1, dc) in last sc changing to Color B in last dc.
Repeat Rows 2-5 until Afghan measures approximately 62", ending by working Row 4.
Last Row: Ch 4, turn; dc in same st, ch 1, (dc in next sc, ch 1) twice, decrease, ch 1, (dc in next sc, ch 1) twice, ★ holding next ch-4 in **back**, work (2 dc, ch 2, 2 dc) in ch-3 sp one row **below** ch-4, ch 1, (dc in next sc, ch 1) twice, decrease, ch 1, (dc in next sc, ch 1) twice; repeat from ★ across to last sc, (dc, ch 1, dc) in last sc; finish off.
Top Edging: With **right** side facing and working across Last Row, join Color A with slip st in first dc; ch 1, skip first ch-1 sp, (slip st in next ch-1 sp, ch 1) 6 times, skip next dc, slip st in next dc, ch 1, ★ slip st in next ch-2 sp, ch 1, slip st in next dc, ch 1, (slip st in next ch-1 sp, ch 1) 6 times, skip next dc, slip st in next dc; repeat from ★ across; finish off.

Bottom Edging: With **right** side facing and working in free loops of beginning ch *(Fig. 27b, page 124)*, join Color A with slip st in first ch; ch 1, (skip next ch, slip st in next ch, ch 1) 3 times, slip st in next ch-2 sp, ch 1, slip st in next ch, (ch 1, skip next ch, slip st in next ch) twice, ★ ch 1, skip next ch, slip st in next 2 chs, ch 1, skip next ch, (slip st in next ch, ch 1, skip next ch) 3 times, slip st in next ch-2 sp, ch 1, slip st in next ch, (ch 1, skip next ch, slip st in next ch) twice; repeat from ★ 8 times **more**, ch 1, skip next ch, slip st in next ch; finish off.

Add tassels as desired *(Figs. 30a & b, page 125)*.

47

RAINBOW STRIPES

Designed especially for kids, this rainbow-striped afghan is quick to crochet because you work with two strands of worsted weight yarn held together. The close weave makes it warm and durable, so it's just right for those winter nights spent lounging in front of the television.

Finished Size: Approximately 45" x 60½"

MATERIALS

Worsted Weight Yarn, approximately:
  MC (Grey) - 33 ounces, (940 grams, 2,170 yards)
  Color A (Red) - 3 ounces, (90 grams, 195 yards)
  Color B (Orange) - 3 ounces, (90 grams, 195 yards)
  Color C (Yellow) - 3 ounces, (90 grams, 195 yards)
  Color D (Green) - 3 ounces, (90 grams, 195 yards)
  Color E (Blue) - 3 ounces, (90 grams, 195 yards)
  Color F (Purple) - 3 ounces, (90 grams, 195 yards)
Crochet hook, size N (9.00 mm) **or** size needed for gauge

Note: Entire Afghan is worked holding two strands of yarn together.

GAUGE: In pattern, (sc, ch 1) 5 times and 10 rows = 4"

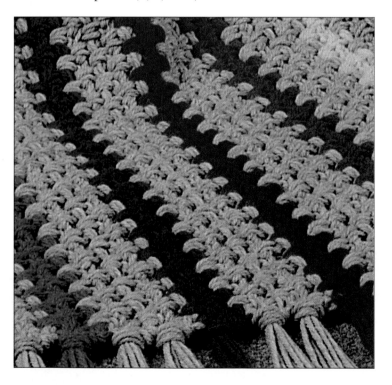

STRIPE SEQUENCE

★ 4 Rows MC *(Fig. 28, page 124)*, 2 rows Color A, 4 rows MC, 2 rows Color B, 4 rows MC, 2 rows Color C, 4 rows MC, 2 rows Color D, 4 rows MC, 2 rows Color E, 4 rows MC, 2 rows Color F; repeat from ★ 2 times **more**, 5 rows MC.

With MC, ch 152 **loosely**.

Row 1 (Right side): Sc in second ch from hook and in each ch across: 151 sc.

Note: Loop a short piece of yarn around any stitch to mark last row as **right** side.

Row 2: Ch 1, turn; sc in first sc, ★ ch 1, skip next sc, sc in next sc; repeat from ★ across: 75 ch-1 sps.

Row 3: Ch 1, turn; sc in first sc and in next ch-1 sp, (ch 1, sc in next ch-1 sp) across, sc in last sc: 74 ch-1 sps.

Row 4: Ch 1, turn; sc in first sc, (ch 1, sc in next ch-1 sp) across to last 2 sc, ch 1, skip next sc, sc in last sc: 75 ch-1 sps.

Rows 5-112: Repeat Rows 3 and 4, 54 times.

Row 113: Ch 1, turn; sc in first sc, sc in each ch-1 sp and in each sc across; finish off.

Add fringe in every other row across *(Figs. 31b & d, page 126)*.

REALLY RED

This apple-red afghan will bring a harvest of color wherever it's used! Quick to crochet using two strands of yarn held together, the lacy panels are created with simple V-stitches. A long, flowing fringe enhances the dramatic look.

Finished Size: Approximately 51" x 67"

MATERIALS
Worsted Weight Yarn, approximately:
 59 ounces, (1,680 grams, 4,045 yards)
Crochet hook, size N (9.00 mm) **or** size needed for
 gauge

Note #1: Entire Afghan is worked holding two strands of
 yarn together.
Note #2: Afghan is worked from side to side.

GAUGE: 9 sc and 10 rows = 4"

Ch 152 **loosely.**
Row 1 (Right side): Sc in second ch from hook and in each ch across: 151 sc.
Note: Loop a short piece of yarn around any stitch to mark last row as **right** side.
Rows 2-4: Ch 1, turn; sc in each sc across.
Note: To work **V-St**, (dc, ch 2, dc) in st or sp indicated.
Row 5: Ch 5 **(counts as first dc plus ch 2, now and throughout),** turn; dc in same st **(counts as first V-St),** (skip next 2 sc, work V-St in next sc) across: 51 V-Sts.
Rows 6-8: Ch 5, turn; dc in first ch-2 sp, work V-St in next ch-2 sp and in each ch-2 sp across.
Row 9: Ch 1, turn; sc in first ch-2 sp, ★ sc in next dc, skip next dc, 2 sc in next ch-2 sp; repeat from ★ across: 151 sc.
Rows 10-12: Ch 1, turn; sc in each sc across.
Row 13: Ch 6, turn; skip first 2 sc, slip st in next sc, ★ ch 6, skip next sc, slip st in next sc; repeat from ★ across to last 2 sc, ch 3, skip next sc, dc in last sc to form last loop: 75 loops.
Row 14: Ch 1, turn; 2 sc in same loop, ch 1, (sc in next loop, ch 1) across to last loop, 2 sc in last loop: 151 sts.
Row 15: Ch 1, turn; sc in each sc and in each ch-1 sp across.
Rows 16-96: Repeat Rows 2-15, 5 times; then repeat Rows 2-12 once **more.**
Finish off.

Add fringe **(Figs. 31b & d, page 126).**

SUNNY AND WARM

*Bold as a field of sunflowers, this granny square afghan will bring the
warmth of summer to any season. The sunny squares are extra easy
to make using a jumbo hook and holding two strands of yarn together.*

Finished Size: Approximately 52" x 69"

MATERIALS
Worsted Weight Yarn, approximately:
   MC (Green) - 38 ounces,
     (1,080 grams, 2,605 yards)
   Color A (Brown) - 11¹/2 ounces,
     (330 grams, 790 yards)
   Color B (Gold) - 10¹/2 ounces,
     (300 grams, 720 yards)
   Crochet hook, size P (10.00 mm) **or** size needed for
   gauge

Note: Entire Afghan is worked holding two strands of
   yarn together.

GAUGE: One Square = 8"

SQUARE (Make 48)
With Color A, ch 5; join with slip st to form a ring.
Rnd 1 (Right side): Ch 3 **(counts as first dc, now and
throughout)**, 15 dc in ring; join with slip st to first dc:
16 dc.
Note: Loop a short piece of yarn around any stitch to mark
last round as **right** side.
Rnd 2: Ch 4, (dc in next dc, ch 1) around; join with slip st
to third ch of beginning ch-4, finish off: 16 ch-1 sps.
Rnd 3: With **right** side facing, join Color B with slip st in
any ch-1 sp; ch 3, dc in same sp, ch 1, (2 dc in next
ch-1 sp, ch 1) around; join with slip st to first dc, finish off:
32 dc.
Rnd 4: With **right** side facing, join MC with slip st in any
ch-1 sp; ch 1, sc in same sp, ch 5, (sc in next ch-1 sp, ch 3)
3 times, ★ sc in next ch-1 sp, ch 5, (sc in next ch-1 sp,
ch 3) 3 times; repeat from ★ around; join with slip st to
first sc: 16 sps.

Rnd 5: Slip st in first ch-5 sp, ch 3, (4 dc, tr, 5 dc) in same
sp, 2 dc in each of next 3 ch-3 sps, ★ (5 dc, tr, 5 dc) in
next ch-5 sp, 2 dc in each of next 3 ch-3 sps; repeat from
★ around; join with slip st to first dc, finish off:
16 dc **each** side.

ASSEMBLY
Afghan is assembled by joining Squares together, forming
6 vertical strips of 8 Squares each and then by joining
strips.
Join Squares as follows: With **right** sides together and
working through outside loops, join MC with slip st in
corner tr; slip st in each st across to next corner tr;
finish off.
Join strips in same manner.

EDGING
Rnd 1: With **right** side facing and working in Back Loops
Only **(Fig. 26, page 124)**, join MC with slip st in any
corner tr; ch 1, 3 sc in same st, sc in next 16 dc, (dc in next
tr, dc in joining and in next tr, sc in next 16 dc) across to
next corner tr, ★ 3 sc in corner tr, sc in next 16 dc, (dc in
next tr, dc in joining and in next tr, sc in next 16 dc)
across to next corner tr; repeat from ★ around; join with
slip st to **both** loops of first sc: 532 sts.
Rnd 2: Ch 3, working in both loops, 3 dc in next sc, ★ dc
in each st across to next corner sc, 3 dc in corner sc; repeat
from ★ 2 times **more**, dc in each st across; join with slip st
to first dc, finish off.

CAMPUS COLORS

Send your favorite student off to college with this smart throw in tow. Crocheted in the university's colors, it'll be a campus sensation! Easy-to-do front post double crochet and V-stitches provide the striped pattern with rich detail.

Finished Size: Approximately 44" x 59"

MATERIALS
Worsted Weight Yarn, approximately:
MC (Ecru) - 18^1/$_2$ ounces,
(530 grams, 1,215 yards)
Color A (Grey) - 8^1/$_2$ ounces,
(240 grams, 560 yards)
Color B (Gold) - 8^1/$_2$ ounces,
(240 grams, 560 yards)
Crochet hook, size J (6.00 mm) **or** size needed for gauge

GAUGE: In pattern, 14 sts and 7 rows = 4"

STRIPE SEQUENCE
6 Rows MC (*Fig. 28, page 124)*, ★ 4 rows Color A,
2 rows MC, 4 rows Color B, 6 rows MC, 4 rows Color B,
2 rows MC, 4 rows Color A, 6 rows MC; repeat from
★ 2 times **more**.

Note: To work **V-St**, (dc, ch 1, dc) in st or sp indicated.

With MC, ch 156 **loosely**.
Row 1: Work V-St in sixth ch from hook, (skip next 2 chs, work V-St in next ch) across to last 3 chs, skip next 2 chs, dc in last ch: 50 V-Sts.
Note: To work **Front Post double crochet (abbreviated FPdc)**, YO, insert hook from **front** to **back** around post of st indicated, YO and pull up a loop even with last st worked (3 loops on hook), (YO and draw through 2 loops on hook) twice, skip st behind FPdc (*Fig. 11, page 119)*.

Row 2 (Right side): Ch 3 **(counts as first dc, now and throughout)**, turn; work FPdc around next dc, dc in next ch-1 sp, ★ work FPdc around each of next 2 dc, dc in next ch-1 sp; repeat from ★ across to last 2 sts, work FPdc around next dc, dc in last st: 152 sts.
Note: Loop a short piece of yarn around any stitch to mark last row as **right** side.
Row 3: Ch 3, turn; skip first FPdc, work V-St in next dc, (skip next 2 FPdc, work V-St in next dc) across to last 2 sts, skip next FPdc, dc in last dc: 50 V-Sts.
Row 4: Ch 3, turn; work FPdc around next dc, dc in next ch-1 sp, ★ work FPdc around each of next 2 dc, dc in next ch-1 sp; repeat from ★ across to last 2 sts, work FPdc around next dc, dc in last dc: 152 sts.
Rows 5-102: Repeat Rows 3 and 4, 49 times.
Do **not** finish off.

EDGING
Rnd 1: Ch 1, do **not** turn; work 203 sc evenly spaced across end of rows; working in free loops of beginning ch (*Fig. 27b, page 124)*, 3 sc in first ch (corner), work 149 sc evenly spaced across to last ch, 3 sc in last ch (corner); work 203 sc evenly spaced across end of rows; working in sts of Row 102, 3 sc in first dc (corner), work 149 sc evenly spaced across to last dc, 3 sc in last dc (corner); join with slip st to first sc: 716 sc.
Rnd 2: Slip st in next sc, ch 2, do **not** turn; ★ working from **left** to **right**, skip next sc, work reverse hdc in next sc (*Figs. 18a-d, page 121)*, ch 1, skip next sc; repeat from ★ around; join with slip st to base of beginning ch-2, finish off.

TRUE BLUE

Bordered with a lacy edging, our bright throw features a handsome pattern of cross stitches set off with openwork. This richly textured afghan will be a true-blue favorite on a chilly winter evening!

Finished Size: Approximately 50" x 67"

MATERIALS
Worsted Weight Yarn, approximately:
43 ounces, (1,220 grams, 2,825 yards)
Crochet hook, size I (5.50 mm) **or** size needed for gauge

GAUGE: In pattern, 4 Cross Sts and 7 rows = 4¹/2"

Ch 173 **loosely**.

Row 1: Skip first 5 chs from hook and dc in next 2 chs, dc in fourth skipped ch and in next skipped ch, (skip next 2 chs, dc in next 2 chs, dc in first skipped ch and in next skipped ch) 5 times, dc in next ch, ★ (ch 1, skip next ch, dc in next ch) twice, (skip next 2 chs, dc in next 2 chs, dc in first skipped ch and in next skipped ch) 6 times, dc in next ch; repeat from ★ across: 161 sts.

Note: To work **Cross St** (uses next 4 dc), skip next 2 dc, dc in next 2 dc, dc in first skipped dc and in next skipped dc **(Figs. 21a & b, page 122)**.

Row 2 (Right side): Ch 3 **(counts as first dc, now and throughout)**, turn; work 6 Cross Sts, ★ dc in next dc, (ch 1, dc in next dc) twice, work 6 Cross Sts; repeat from ★ across, dc in top of beginning ch: 36 Cross Sts.

Note: Loop a short piece of yarn around any stitch to mark last row as **right** side.

Row 3: Ch 3, turn; work 6 Cross Sts, dc in next dc, ★ (ch 1, dc in next dc) twice, work 6 Cross Sts, dc in next dc; repeat from ★ across.

Repeat Row 3 until Afghan measures approximately 65", ending by working a **wrong** side row; do **not** finish off.

EDGING

Rnd 1: Ch 4, turn; (dc, ch 1) twice in same st, skip next st, (dc in next st, ch 1, skip next st) across to last st, (dc, ch 1) 3 times in last st; working in ends of rows, dc in first row, ch 1, [(dc, ch 1) twice in next row, dc in next row, ch 1] across; working in free loops of beginning ch **(Fig. 27b, page 124)**, (dc, ch 1) 3 times in first ch, skip next ch, (dc in next ch, ch 1, skip next ch) across to last ch, (dc, ch 1) 3 times in last ch; working in ends of rows, dc in first row, ch 1, [(dc, ch 1) twice in next row, dc in next row, ch 1] across; join with slip st to third ch of beginning ch-4.

Rnd 2: Ch 1, do **not** turn; sc in same st, ch 3, (sc in next dc, ch 3) around; join with slip st to first sc, finish off.

MERRY AND BRIGHT

Even if Christmas is just around the corner, you'll still have time to make this festive afghan for a special gift. Its mile-a-minute design works up so quickly, you may want to crochet two — one to keep and one to give. What an easy way to make the holidays merry and bright!

Finished Size: Approximately 45" x 61"

MATERIALS
Worsted Weight Yarn, approximately:
MC (Variegated) - 20 ounces,
(570 grams, 1,315 yards)
Color A (Red) - 7 ounces, (200 grams, 460 yards)
Color B (Green) - 7 ounces, (200 grams, 460 yards)
Color C (White) - 6 ounces,
(170 grams, 395 yards)
Crochet hooks, sizes G (4.00 mm) **and** H (5.00 mm)
or sizes needed for gauge

GAUGE: With larger size hook,
Center Shells (before Edging) = 2" wide
11 rows = 8"
With smaller size hook,
11 3-dc groups = 8"

SHELL STRIP (Make 14)
CENTER SHELLS
With larger size hook and MC, ch 6; join with slip st to form a ring.
Row 1 (Right side): Ch 3, (2 dc, ch 2, 3 dc) in ring.
Note: Loop a short piece of yarn around any stitch to mark last row as **right** side and bottom edge.
Rows 2-80: Ch 3, turn; (3 dc, ch 2, 3 dc) in ch-2 sp, dc in top of beginning ch-3.
Finish off.

EDGING
Note: To work **double treble crochet (abbreviated dtr)**, YO 3 times, insert hook in sp indicated, YO and pull up a loop (5 loops on hook), (YO and draw through 2 loops on hook) 4 times **(Figs. 8a & b, page 118)**.
Rnd 1: With **right** side facing and smaller size hook, join Color A with slip st in beginning ring; ch 5, 14 dtr in same sp, skip end of first row, work 3 dc in end of each row across, 15 dtr in next ch-2 sp, work 3 dc in end each row across to last row, skip last row; join with slip st to top of beginning ch-5, finish off: 79 3-dc groups **each** side.
Repeat on 6 **more** Strips (7 Strips total); then repeat on 7 remaining Strips, substituting Color B for Color A.

ASSEMBLY
With **right** side facing and smaller size hook, join Color C with slip st in first dc at top of any Color A Strip; ch 1, sc in same st, ch 2; having any Color B Strip adjacent and top at same end, sc in first dc on Color B Strip, ★ ch 2, skip next dc on Color A Strip, sc in next dc on Color A Strip, ch 2, skip next dc on Color B Strip, sc in next dc on Color B Strip; repeat from ★ across; finish off.
Join remaining Strips in same manner, alternating Color A and Color B Strips.

BORDER
With **right** side facing and smaller size hook, join Color C with slip st in any st, ch 1; working from **left** to **right**, work reverse sc in each st around **(Figs. 17a-d, page 121)**; join with slip st to first st, finish off.

PRIMARY FUN

Crocheted in bright primary colors, this cozy cover-up will be a hit with kids. They'll love wrapping up in it while they sample an after-school snack — and it may even make homework more enjoyable! Our fun afghan earns top grades for being simple to make, too. You'll have the ten easy strips crocheted and joined together before you know it!

Finished Size: Approximately 50" x 70"

MATERIALS

Worsted Weight Yarn, approximately:
- Color A (Black) - 11 ounces, (310 grams, 725 yards)
- Color B (Red) - 10 ounces, (280 grams, 660 yards)
- Color C (Blue) - 10 ounces, (280 grams, 660 yards)
- Color D (Yellow) - 10 ounces, (280 grams, 660 yards)
- Color E (Green) - 9 ounces, (260 grams, 595 yards)

Crochet hook, size H (5.00 mm) **or** size needed for gauge

Yarn needle

GAUGE: 14 dc and 7 rows = 4"
One Strip = 5" wide

STRIP (Make 10)

With Color D, ch 7 **loosely**.

Row 1 (Right side): Dc in fourth ch from hook and in each ch across: 5 sts.

Note: Loop a short piece of yarn around any stitch to mark last row as **right** side and bottom edge.

Row 2: Ch 3 **(counts as first dc, now and throughout)**, turn; dc in next dc and in each st across: 5 dc.

Rows 3-113: Ch 3, turn; dc in next dc and in each dc across.
Finish off.

Note: Begin working in rounds.

Rnd 1: With **right** side facing and working across Row 113, skip first 2 dc and join Color C with slip st in next dc; ch 3, 4 dc in same st, skip last 2 dc; † working in end of rows, 3 dc in first row, 2 dc in next row and in each row across to last row, 3 dc in last row †; working in free loops of beginning ch **(Fig. 27b, page 124)**, skip first 2 chs, 5 dc in next ch, skip next 2 chs, repeat from † to † once; join with slip st to first dc, finish off: 466 dc.

Rnd 2: With **right** side facing, join Color B with slip st in center dc of any 5-dc group; ch 3, 6 dc in same st, † skip next 2 dc, 4 dc in sp **before** next dc, skip next 3 dc, dc in sp **before** next dc, place marker around dc just made to mark Trim placement, dc in same sp, (skip next 2 dc, 2 dc in sp **before** next dc) 111 times, skip next 3 dc, 4 dc in sp **before** next dc, skip next 2 dc †, 7 dc in next dc, repeat from † to † once; join with slip st to first dc, finish off: 478 dc.

TRIM

With **right** side facing, join Color E with slip st in sp **before** marked dc; ch 3, dc in same sp, (skip next 2 dc, 2 dc in sp **before** next dc) 112 times; finish off: 226 dc.
Repeat across second side.

EDGING

With **right** side facing, join Color A with slip st in center dc of any 7-dc group on Rnd 2; ch 4, (2 tr, ch 1, 3 tr) in same st, † skip next 3 dc, (4 dc in sp **before** next dc, skip next 2 dc) twice, 2 dc in end of Trim; working across Trim, dc in first dc and in each dc across, 2 dc in end of Trim; working across Rnd 2, skip first 2 dc, 4 dc in sp **before** next dc, skip next 2 dc, 4 dc in sp **before** next dc, skip next 3 dc †, (3 tr, ch 1, 3 tr) in next dc, repeat from † to † once; join with slip st to top of beginning ch-4, finish off.

ASSEMBLY

With **wrong** side of two Strips together, bottom edges at the same end and using Color A, whipstitch Strips together working through **both** loops of dc across side of Strip only **(Fig. 29b, page 125)**.

Join remaining Strips in same manner, always working in the same direction.

THE RED, WHITE, AND BLUE

Clusters of red, white, and blue turn this traditional ripple afghan into a patriotic pleaser! Perfect for Flag Day or the Fourth of July, this all-American charmer is quick and easy to create because you work with two strands of yarn held together.

Finished Size: Approximately 45" x 63"

MATERIALS
Worsted Weight Yarn, approximately:
Color A (Blue) - 27 ounces,
(770 grams, 1,850 yards)
Color B (Red) - 18 ounces,
(510 grams, 1,235 yards)
Color C (Ecru) - 16½ ounces,
(470 grams, 1,130 yards)
Crochet hook, size N (9.00 mm) **or** size needed for gauge

Note: Entire Afghan is worked holding two strands of yarn together.

GAUGE: In pattern, 9 sc and 5 rows = 5"
(7½" point to point)

STRIPE SEQUENCE
5 Rows Color A *(Fig. 28, page 124)*, ★ 2 rows Color C, 4 rows Color B, 2 rows Color C, 4 rows Color A; repeat from ★ for sequence.

With Color A, ch 141 **loosely**.
Row 1 (Right side)**:** Sc in second ch from hook and in each ch across: 140 sc.
Note #1: Loop a short piece of yarn around any stitch to mark last row as **right** side.
Note #2: To work **Cluster**, ★ YO, insert hook in st or sp indicated, YO and pull up a loop, YO and draw through 2 loops on hook; repeat from ★ 2 times **more**, YO and draw through all 4 loops on hook.
Row 2: Ch 3 **(counts as first dc, now and throughout)**, turn; skip next 2 sc, (3 dc in next sc, skip next 2 sc) 3 times, (3 dc, ch 3, 3 dc) in next sc, ★ skip next 2 sc, (3 dc in next sc, skip next 2 sc) twice, work Cluster in next sc, skip next 4 sc, work Cluster in next sc, skip next 2 sc, (3 dc in next sc, skip next 2 sc) twice, (3 dc, ch 3, 3 dc) in next sc; repeat from ★ across to last 12 sc, skip next 2 sc, (3 dc in next sc, skip next 2 sc) 3 times, dc in last sc: 38 3-dc groups.

Note: When instructed to work into a sp on Rows 3-5, work in sp **between** 3-dc groups and Clusters.
Rows 3-5: Ch 3, turn; skip first sp (between first dc and next 3-dc group), 3 dc in each of next 3 sps, (3 dc, ch 3, 3 dc) in next ch-3 sp, ★ 3 dc in each of next 2 sps, work Cluster in next sp, skip next 2 Clusters, work Cluster in next sp, 3 dc in each of next 2 sps, (3 dc, ch 3, 3 dc) in next ch-3 sp; repeat from ★ across to last 4 sps, 3 dc in each of next 3 sps, skip last sp (between next 3-dc group and last dc), dc in last dc: 10 Clusters.
Finish off.
Row 6: With **wrong** side facing, join Color C with slip st in BLO of first dc *(Fig. 26, page 124)*; ch 3, skip next dc, dc in BLO of next 11 dc, 3 dc in next ch-3 sp, ★ dc in BLO of next 9 dc, skip next 2 Clusters, dc in BLO of next 9 dc, 3 dc in next ch-3 sp; repeat from ★ across to last 13 dc, dc in BLO of next 11 dc, skip next dc, dc in BLO of last dc: 132 dc.
Row 7: Ch 3, turn; skip next dc, working in BLO, dc in next 11 dc, 3 dc in next dc, ★ dc in next 9 dc, skip next 2 dc, dc in next 9 dc, 3 dc in next dc; repeat from ★ across to last 13 dc, dc in next 11 dc, skip next dc, dc in last dc; finish off.
Row 8: With **wrong** side facing and working in both loops, join next color with slip st in first dc; ch 3, skip next 3 dc, (3 dc in next dc, skip next 2 dc) 3 times, (3 dc, ch 3, 3 dc) in next dc, ★ skip next 2 dc, (3 dc in next dc, skip next 2 dc) twice, (work Cluster in next dc, skip next 2 dc) twice, (3 dc in next dc, skip next 2 dc) twice, (3 dc, ch 3, 3 dc) in next dc; repeat from ★ across to last 13 dc, (skip next 2 dc, 3 dc in next dc) 3 times, skip next 3 dc, dc in last dc: 38 3-dc groups.
Repeat Rows 3-8 until Afghan measures approximately 62½", ending by working Row 5 with Color A.
Do **not** finish off.
Last Row: Ch 1, turn; sc in first 13 dc, 3 sc in next ch-3 sp, ★ sc in next 9 dc, skip next 2 Clusters, sc in next 9 dc, 3 sc in next ch-3 sp; repeat from ★ across to last 13 dc, sc in last 13 dc; finish off.

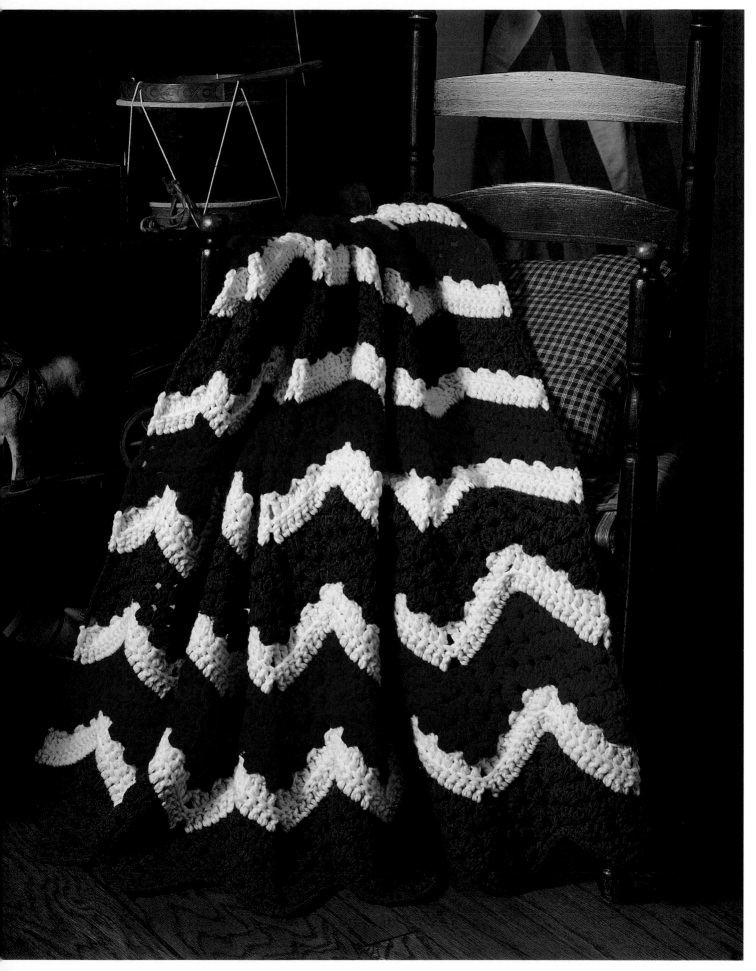

CLASSIC ELEGANCE

Elegance never goes out of fashion, and this unforgettable array includes afghans with a timeless look. Easy to crochet in luxuriously muted shades, our wraps feature classic designs befitting a formal living room, den, or library. Many use traditional pattern stitches — shells, popcorns, puffs, and more — that will lavish your distinguished rooms with rich texture. With such a stylish collection, you'll enjoy draping your home in the handmade finery of these gorgeous throws.

SOPHISTICATED SWIRL

This snow-white afghan is aswirl with style! The pretty pinwheel motifs, fashioned with single crochet stitches and chain spaces, work up quickly because you use two strands of yarn. Whipstitched together, they form a simply stunning throw.

Finished Size: Approximately 45" x 61"

MATERIALS
Worsted Weight Yarn, approximately:
   51 ounces, (1,450 grams, 2,975 yards)
Crochet hook, size N (9.00 mm) **or** size needed for
   gauge
Yarn needle

Note: Entire Afghan is worked holding two strands of
   yarn together.

GAUGE: One Motif = 10"
   (from straight edge to straight edge)

MOTIF (Make 27)
Ch 5; join with slip st to form a ring.
Rnd 1 (Right side): Ch 1, (sc in ring, ch 2) 6 times; join with slip st to first sc: 6 ch-2 sps.
Note: Loop a short piece of yarn around any stitch to mark last round as **right** side.
Rnd 2: Slip st in first ch-2 sp, ch 1, sc in same sp and in next sc, ch 3, ★ sc in next ch-2 sp and in next sc, ch 3; repeat from ★ 3 times **more**, sc in next ch-2 sp and in same st as joining, ch 3; join with slip st to first sc: 12 sc.
Note: Markers are used to help distinguish the beginning of each round being worked. Place a 2" scrap piece of yarn before the first stitch of each round, moving marker after each round is complete.
Rnd 3: Ch 3, skip next sc, 2 sc in first ch-3 sp, ★ sc in next sc, ch 3, skip next sc, 2 sc in next ch-3 sp; repeat from ★ around, sc in same st as joining; do **not** join, place marker: 18 sc.
Rnd 4: Ch 3, 2 sc in next ch-3 sp, sc in next 2 sc, ★ ch 3, skip next sc, 2 sc in next ch-3 sp, sc in next 2 sc; repeat from ★ 4 times **more**: 24 sc.

Rnd 5: ★ Ch 3, skip next sc, 2 sc in next ch-3 sp, sc in next 3 sc; repeat from ★ 5 times **more**: 30 sc.
Rnd 6: ★ Ch 3, skip next sc, 2 sc in next ch-3 sp, sc in next 4 sc; repeat from ★ 5 times **more**: 36 sc.
Rnd 7: ★ Ch 3, skip next sc, 2 sc in next ch-3 sp, sc in next 5 sc; repeat from ★ 5 times **more**: 42 sc.
Rnd 8: ★ Ch 3, skip next sc, 2 sc in next ch-3 sp, sc in next 6 sc; repeat from ★ 5 times **more**: 48 sc.
Rnd 9: ★ Ch 3, skip next sc, 2 sc in next ch-3 sp, sc in next 7 sc; repeat from ★ 5 times **more**: 54 sc.
Rnd 10: ★ Ch 4, skip next sc, 2 sc in next ch-3 sp, sc in next 8 sc; repeat from ★ 5 times **more**; slip st in next sc, finish off: 60 sc.

ASSEMBLY
With **wrong** sides together and working through inside loops, whipstitch Motifs together, forming 3 vertical strips of 5 Motifs each and 2 vertical strips of 6 Motifs each (*Fig. 29a, page 125*); then whipstitch strips together, alternating strips of 5-6-5-6-5 Motifs.

EDGING
Rnd 1: With **right** side facing, join yarn with slip st in any sc; ch 1, sc in each sc around working 4 sc in each ch-4 sp and 2 sc in each ch-2 sp at joining; join with slip st to first sc.
Rnd 2: Ch 1, hdc in same st, ch 1; working from left to right, skip next sc, ★ work reverse hdc in next sc (*Figs. 18a-d, page 121*), ch 1, skip next sc; repeat from ★ around; join with slip st to first hdc, finish off.

VICTORIAN HEIRLOOM

Destined to become an heirloom, this puff stitch afghan has a lovely old-fashioned look. Its intricate pattern is showcased in lush teal brushed acrylic yarn, and a scalloped edging adds a touch of elegance.

Finished Size: Approximately 49" x 65"

MATERIALS
Worsted Weight Yarn, approximately:
69 ounces, (1,960 grams, 4,340 yards)
Crochet hook, size I (5.50 mm) **or** size needed for gauge

GAUGE: [(Sc, ch 2, sc) in next ch-4 sp, ch 4] 3 times and 7 rows = 3¹/₂"

Note: To work **Puff St**, (YO, insert hook in sp indicated, YO and pull up a loop even with st on hook) 4 times, YO and draw through 8 loops on hook, YO and draw through remaining 2 loops on hook.

Ch 173 **loosely**.
Row 1: Sc in ninth ch from hook, (ch 4, skip next 3 chs, sc in next ch) across: 42 sps.
Row 2 (Right side): Ch 5, turn; (sc, ch 2, sc) in first ch-4 sp, ch 4, ★ (sc, ch 2, sc) in next ch-4 sp, ch 4; repeat from ★ across to last sp, sc in last sp.
Note: Loop a short piece of yarn around any stitch to mark last row as **right** side.
Row 3: Ch 5, turn; (sc, ch 2, sc) in first ch-4 sp, ch 4, skip next ch-2 sp, sc in next ch-4 sp, work (Puff St, ch 2, Puff St) in next ch-2 sp, ★ sc in next ch-4 sp, ch 4, skip next ch-2 sp, (sc, ch 2, sc) in next ch-4 sp, ch 4, skip next ch-2 sp, sc in next ch-4 sp, work (Puff St, ch 2, Puff St) in next ch-2 sp; repeat from ★ across to last sp, sc in last sp.
Row 4: Ch 5, turn; work [Puff St, (ch 2, Puff St) twice] in next ch-2 sp, ch 3, sc in next ch-4 sp, ch 4, ★ skip next ch-2 sp, sc in next ch-4 sp, ch 3, work [Puff St, (ch 2, Puff St) 4 times] in next ch-2 sp, ch 3, sc in next ch-4 sp, ch 4; repeat from ★ across to last 2 sps, skip next ch-2 sp, sc in last sp.
Row 5: Ch 5, turn; (sc, ch 2, sc) in first ch-4 sp, ch 4, ★ skip next ch-3 sp, sc in next ch-2 sp, (ch 3, sc in next ch-2 sp) 3 times, ch 4, skip next ch-3 sp, (sc, ch 2, sc) in next ch-4 sp, ch 4; repeat from ★ across to last 4 sps, skip next ch-3 sp, (sc in next ch-2 sp, ch 3) twice, sc in last sp.

Row 6: Ch 5, turn; (sc, ch 2, sc) in first ch-3 sp, ch 4, skip next ch-3 sp, (sc, ch 2, sc) in next ch-4 sp, ch 4, ★ skip next ch-2 sp, (sc, ch 2, sc) in next ch-4 sp, ch 4, skip next ch-3 sp, (sc, ch 2, sc) in next ch-3 sp, ch 4, skip next ch-3 sp, (sc, ch 2, sc) in next ch-4 sp, ch 4; repeat from ★ across to last 2 sps, skip next ch-2 sp, sc in last sp.
Row 7: Ch 5, turn; (sc, ch 2, sc) in first ch-4 sp, ch 4, ★ skip next ch-2 sp, (sc, ch 2, sc) in next ch-4 sp, ch 4; repeat from ★ across to last 2 sps, skip next ch-2 sp, sc in last sp.
Rows 8-106: Repeat Rows 3-7, 19 times; then repeat Rows 3-6 once **more**.
Row 107: Ch 4; turn; sc in first ch-4 sp, ch 4, ★ skip next ch-2 sp, sc in next ch-4 sp, ch 4; repeat from ★ across to last 2 sps, skip next ch-2 sp, sc in last sp; do **not** finish off: 42 ch-4 sps.

EDGING
FIRST SHORT END
Row 1: Ch 5, turn; sc in first ch-4 sp, ch 16 **loosely**, sc in back ridge of fifth ch from hook and in each ch across *(Fig. 2b, page 117)*, sc in same sp, ch 1, ★ (sc, ch 5, sc) in next ch-4 sp, ch 1, sc in next ch-4 sp, ch 16 **loosely**, sc in back ridge of fifth ch from hook and in each ch across, sc in same sp, ch 1; repeat from ★ across to last sp, (sc, ch 5, sc) in last sp: 21 points.
Note: To work **Extended Puff St** (uses next 3 sts), ★ working in **next** st [(YO, insert hook in st, YO and pull up a loop even with st on hook) twice]; repeat from ★ 2 times **more**, YO and draw through 12 loops on hook, YO and draw through remaining 2 loops on hook.
Row 2: Ch 2, turn; sc in first ch-5 sp, ★ ch 2, skip next 2 sc, working in sc on next point, work (Extended Puff St, ch 2) 4 times, in ch-4 sp at top of same point work [dc, (ch 1, dc) 4 times], ch 2, working in free loops of remaining 12 chs of ch-16 *(Fig. 27b, page 124)*, work (Extended Puff St, ch 2) 4 times, sc in next ch-5 sp; repeat from ★ across.

Row 3 (Joining row): Ch 3, turn; skip first ch-2 sp, (sc in next ch-2 sp, ch 3) 4 times, (sc in next ch-1 sp, ch 3) 4 times, (sc in next ch-2 sp, ch 3) 3 times, sc in next ch-2 sp, ch 2, ★ skip next ch-2 sp, sc in next sc, ch 2, skip next ch-2 sp, sc in next ch-2 sp on **next** point, ch 2, skip last 2 ch-2 sps made, sc in next ch-3 sp on **last** point, ch 1, sc in next ch-2 sp on **next** point, (ch 2, sc in next ch-3 sp on **last** point, ch 1, sc in next ch-2 sp on **next** point) twice, ch 3, (sc in next ch-1 sp, ch 3) 4 times, (sc in next ch-2 sp, ch 3) 3 times, sc in next ch-2 sp, ch 2; repeat from ★ across to last 2 sps, skip next ch-2 sp, sc in last sp; finish off.

SECOND SHORT END

Row 1: With **right** side facing and working over beginning ch, join yarn with slip st in first sp; ch 5, sc in same sp, ch 16 **loosely**, sc in back ridge of fifth ch from hook and in each ch across, sc in same sp, ch 1, ★ (sc, ch 5, sc) in next sp, ch 1, sc in next sp, ch 16 **loosely**, sc in back ridge of fifth ch from hook and in each ch across, sc in same sp, ch 1; repeat from ★ across to last sp, (sc, ch 5, sc) in last sp: 21 points.

Complete same as First Short End.

UNDERSTATED ELEGANCE

*An old favorite is given sophisticated style in this mile-a-minute granny afghan.
It's worked in strips of shell stitches, with variegated yarn adding a textured look.
The matching pillow features granny triangles joined using reverse single crochet.*

Finished Size:
Afghan: Approximately 45" x 60"
Pillow: Approximately 16" x 16"

MATERIALS
Worsted Weight Yarn, approximately:
MC (Variegated)- 16 ounces, (450 grams, 1,050 yards)
Color A (Plum) - 9 ounces, (260 grams, 590 yards)
Color B (Mauve) - 13³/4 ounces, (390 grams, 905 yards)
Color C (Taupe) - 10¹/2 ounces, (300 grams, 690 yards)
Crochet hooks, sizes G (4.00 mm) **and** H (5.00 mm)
or sizes needed for gauge
Square pillow form - 16" x 16"
1¹/8" Button - 2
Tapestry needle

AFGHAN

GAUGE: With larger size hook,
Center Shells (before Edging) = 2" wide
11 rows = 8"
With smaller size hook, 11 3-dc groups = 8"

SHELL STRIP (Make 10)
CENTER SHELLS
With larger size hook and MC, ch 6; join with slip st to
form a ring.
Row 1 (Right side): Ch 3 **(counts as first dc, now and
throughout)**, (2 dc, ch 2, 3 dc) in ring.
Note: Loop a short piece of yarn around any stitch to mark
last row as **right** side and bottom edge.
Rows 2-78: Ch 3, turn; (3 dc, ch 2, 3 dc) in ch-2 sp, dc in
last dc.
Finish off.

EDGING
Rnd 1: With **right** side facing and smaller size hook, join
Color A with slip st in beginning ring; ch 3, (2 dc, ch 1,
3 dc) in same sp **(beginning Shell made)**; working in end of
rows, skip first row, (2 dc, ch 1, 2 dc) in next row **(Corner
Shell made)**, work 3 dc in each row across to last row, work
Corner Shell in last row, (3 dc, ch 1, 3 dc) in next ch-2 sp
(Shell made); working in end of rows, work Corner Shell
in first row, work 3 dc in each row across to last 2 rows,

work Corner Shell in next row, skip last row; join with
slip st to first dc, finish off: 75 3-dc groups **each** side.
Rnd 2: With **wrong** side facing and smaller size hook, join
Color B with slip st in ch-1 sp of beginning Shell; ch 3,
work beginning Shell in same sp, † 3 dc in next sp, work
Corner Shell in next Corner Shell (ch-1 sp), 3 dc in each
sp across to next Corner Shell, work Corner Shell in
Corner Shell, 3 dc in next sp †, work Shell in next Shell
(ch-1 sp), repeat from † to † once; join with slip st to first
dc, finish off: 76 3-dc groups **each** side.
Rnd 3: With **right** side facing and smaller size hook, join
Color C with slip st in ch-1 sp of beginning Shell; ch 3,
work beginning Shell in same sp, † 3 dc in each of next
2 sps, work Corner Shell in next Corner Shell, 3 dc in each
sp across to next Corner Shell, work Corner Shell in
Corner Shell, 3 dc in each of next 2 sps †, work Shell in
next Shell, repeat from † to † once; join with slip st to first
dc, finish off: 77 3-dc groups **each** side.

ASSEMBLY
With **wrong** side of two Strips together, bottom edges at
same end and using smaller size hook, join Color B with
slip st in ch-1 sp of Corner Shell, ch 1; working from **left** to
right and working through inside loops across side of both
Strips, work reverse sc in each st across to ch-1 sp of next
Corner Shell **(Figs. 17a-d, page 121)**; finish off.
Join remaining Strips in same manner.

EDGING
With **right** side facing and smaller size hook, join Color B
with slip st in any st, ch 1; working from **left** to **right**, work
reverse sc in each st around; join with slip st to first st,
finish off.

PILLOW

GAUGE: With larger size hook, Rows 1-3 = 2"

GRANNY TRIANGLE (Make 8)
Row 1 (Right side): With larger size hook and MC, ch 4,
6 dc in fourth ch from hook: 7 sts.
Note: Mark last row as **right** side.
Row 2: Ch 3 **(counts as first dc, now and throughout)**,
turn; 2 dc in same st, skip next 2 dc, work Shell in next dc,
skip next 2 dc, 3 dc in top of beginning ch: 12 dc.

Row 3: Ch 3, turn; 2 dc in same st, 3 dc in next sp, work Shell in next Shell, 3 dc in next sp, 3 dc in last dc: 18 dc.

Row 4: Ch 3, turn; 2 dc in same st, 3 dc in each sp across to next Shell, work Shell in Shell, 3 dc in each sp across, 3 dc in last dc: 24 dc.

Rows 5-8: Repeat Row 4, 4 times changing to Color A at end of Row 8 *(Fig. 28, page 124)*: 48 dc.

Note: Begin working in the following color sequence: One row Color A, one row Color B, and one row Color C.

Rows 9-11: Repeat Row 4, 3 times: 66 dc.

Finish off.

ASSEMBLY

Front: Make a large square, joining 4 Triangles as follows: With **wrong** side of two Triangles together, matching Shells and using larger size hook, join Color B with slip st in ch-1 sp of Shell; ch 1, working through inside loops of both pieces, work reverse sc in each st across; finish off. Repeat with remaining Triangles.

Back: Work same as Front.

EDGING

With **wrong** side of Front and Back together, working through both pieces, matching rows and using larger size hook, join Color B with slip st in end of any row; ch 1, (sc, ch 3, dc) in same row and in end of each row around, inserting pillow form before closing; join with slip st to first sc, finish off.

Using tapestry needle, sew buttons in center of both sides of Pillow, sewing through pillow form.

PRECIOUS PEARLS

Wrap yourself in luxury with this exquisite throw featuring ripples of popcorn stitch "pearls." Worked using double strands of creamy worsted weight yarn, it's as lovely as a string of the lustrous jewels.

Finished Size: Approximately 44" x 59"

MATERIALS
Worsted Weight Yarn, approximately:
  56 ounces, (1,590 grams, 3,680 yards)
Crochet hook, size N (9.00 mm) **or** size needed for gauge

Note: Entire Afghan is worked holding two strands of yarn together.

GAUGE: In pattern, 7 sc and 5 rows = 3"
  (6¼" point to point)

PATTERN STITCHES
DECREASE (uses next 2 sts)
★ YO, insert hook in **next** st, YO and pull up a loop, YO and draw through 2 loops on hook; repeat from ★ once **more**, YO and draw through all 3 loops on hook (**counts as one dc**).
POPCORN
4 Dc in st indicated, drop loop from hook, insert hook in first dc of 4-dc group, hook dropped loop and draw through **(Fig. 9b, page 119)**.

Ch 148 **loosely**.
Row 1: Sc in second ch from hook, skip next ch, sc in next 8 chs, 3 sc in next ch, ★ sc in next 9 chs, skip next 2 chs, sc in next 9 chs, 3 sc in next ch; repeat from ★ across to last 10 chs, sc in next 8 chs, skip next ch, sc in last ch: 147 sc.
Row 2 (Right side): Ch 1, turn; working in Back Loops Only **(Fig. 26, page 124)**, sc in first sc, skip next sc, sc in next 8 sc, 3 sc in next sc, ★ sc in next 9 sc, skip next 2 sc, sc in next 9 sc, 3 sc in next sc; repeat from ★ across to last 10 sc, sc in next 8 sc, skip next sc, sc in last sc.
Note: Loop a short piece of yarn around any stitch to mark last row as **right** side.
Rows 3-5: Repeat Row 2, 3 times.

Row 6: Ch 3 (**counts as first dc**), turn; working in Back Loops Only, decrease, dc in next sc, work Popcorn in next sc, dc in next 3 sc, work Popcorn in next sc, dc in next sc, 3 dc in next sc, dc in next sc, ★ (work Popcorn in next sc, dc in next 3 sc) twice, skip next 2 sc, (dc in next 3 sc, work Popcorn in next sc) twice, dc in next sc, 3 dc in next sc, dc in next sc; repeat from ★ across to last 9 sc, work Popcorn in next sc, dc in next 3 sc, work Popcorn in next sc, dc in next sc, decrease, dc in last sc: 28 Popcorns.
Row 7: Ch 1, turn; sc in Back Loop Only of first dc, skip next dc, sc in Back Loop Only of next dc, ★ † sc in **both** loops of next Popcorn, sc in Back Loop Only of next 3 dc, sc in **both** loops of next Popcorn, sc in Back Loop Only of next 2 dc, 3 sc in Back Loop Only of next dc, sc in Back Loop Only of next 2 dc, sc in **both** loops of next Popcorn, sc in Back Loop Only of next 3 dc, sc in **both** loops of next Popcorn †, sc in Back Loop Only of next 2 dc, skip next 2 dc, sc in Back Loop Only of next 2 dc; repeat from ★ 5 times **more**, then repeat from † to † once, sc in Back Loop Only of next dc, skip next dc, sc in Back Loop Only of last dc: 147 sc.
Rows 8-11: Ch 1, turn; working in Back Loops Only, sc in first sc, skip next sc, sc in next 8 sc, 3 sc in next sc, ★ sc in next 9 sc, skip next 2 sc, sc in next 9 sc, 3 sc in next sc; repeat from ★ across to last 10 sc, sc in next 8 sc, skip next sc, sc in last sc.
Repeat Rows 6-11 until Afghan measures approximately 59", ending by working Row 11.
Finish off.

LOVELY RIPPLES

Draped across a chair, this luxurious afghan has the tranquil look of a cascade of rippling water. Quick to work with two strands of yarn held together, it features rows of basic single crochet stitches combined with easy-to-do puff stitches.

Finished Size: Approximately 49" x 65"

MATERIALS
Worsted Weight Yarn, approximately:
70 ounces, (1,990 grams, 4,600 yards)
Crochet hook, size N (9.00 mm) **or** size needed for gauge

Note: Entire Afghan is worked holding two strands of yarn together.

GAUGE: In pattern, 10 sc = 4" and 6 rows = 3¹/₂"
(7" point to point)

Ch 160 **loosely**.

Row 1 (Right side): Sc in second ch from hook and in next 9 chs, 3 sc in next ch, sc in next 10 chs, ★ skip next 2 chs, sc in next 10 chs, 3 sc in next ch, sc in next 10 chs; repeat from ★ across: 161 sc.

Note: Loop a short piece of yarn around any stitch to mark last row as **right** side.

Rows 2-5: Ch 1, turn; working in Back Loops Only **(Fig. 26, page 124)**, pull up a loop in first 2 sts, YO and draw through all 3 loops on hook, sc in next 9 sc, 3 sc in next sc, ★ sc in next 10 sc, skip next 2 sc, sc in next 10 sc, 3 sc in next sc; repeat from ★ 5 times **more**, sc in next 9 sc, pull up a loop in last 2 sts, YO and draw through all 3 loops on hook: 161 sts.

Note: To work **Puff St**, (YO, insert hook in sc indicated, YO and pull up a loop even with st on hook) 3 times, YO and draw through all 7 loops on hook **(Fig. 22, page 122)**.

Row 6: Ch 2, turn; working in both loops, skip first st, work Puff St in next sc, (ch 2, skip next sc, work Puff St in next sc) 10 times, ★ ch 1, skip next 2 sc, work Puff St in next sc, (ch 2, skip next sc, work Puff St in next sc) 10 times; repeat from ★ across to last st, hdc in last st: 77 Puff Sts.

Row 7: Ch 1, turn; (sc in next Puff St, sc in next ch-2 sp) 5 times, 3 sc in next Puff St, (sc in next ch-2 sp, sc in next Puff St) 5 times, ★ skip next ch-1 sp, (sc in next Puff St, sc in next ch-2 sp) 5 times, 3 sc in next Puff St, (sc in next ch-2 sp, sc in next Puff St) 5 times; repeat from ★ across, slip st in top of turning ch: 161 sc.

Repeat Rows 2-7 until Afghan measures approximately 65", ending by working Row 5.
Finish off.

SOFT STRIPES

Blended stripes in soft, muted colors make this pretty wrap a classic!
It's worked with easy single crochet stitches using a jumbo hook and six
strands of yarn held together. You'll finish this warm cover-up in no time.

Finished Size: Approximately 49" x 68"

MATERIALS

Worsted Weight Yarn, approximately:
MC (Ecru) - 63 ounces, (1,790 grams, 3,960 yards)
Color A (Green) - 13 ounces,
(370 grams, 815 yards)
Color B (Rose) - 13 ounces, (370 grams, 815 yards)
Color C (Light Rose) - 13 ounces,
(370 grams, 815 yards)
Crochet hook, size Q (15.00 mm) **or** size needed for
gauge

Note: Afghan is worked from side to side holding six
strands of yarn together. Always join yarn and finish off
leaving an 8" length at each end for fringe.

GAUGE: In pattern, 8 sc and 7 rows = 6"

STRIPE SEQUENCE

One row using 6 strands of MC, ★ one row using 3 strands
of MC and 3 strands of Color A, one row using 3 strands of
MC and 3 strands of Color B, one row using 3 strands of
MC and 3 strands of Color C, one row using 6 strands of
MC; repeat from ★ throughout.

Using 6 strands of MC, ch 90 **loosely**; finish off.
Row 1 (Right side)**:** Working in back ridge of each ch
(Fig. 2b, page 117), join MC with slip st in first ch; ch 1,
sc in same st and in each ch across; finish off: 90 sc.
Note: Loop a short piece of yarn around any stitch to mark
last row as **right** side.
Row 2: With **right** side facing and working in Back Loops
Only **(Fig. 26, page 124)**, join next color(s) with slip st in
first sc; ch 1, sc in same st and in each sc across; finish off.
Repeat Row 2 until Afghan measures approximately 49",
ending by working with 6 strands of MC.

Add additional fringe across both ends of Afghan
(Figs. 31b & d, page 126).

CLASSIC TEXTURE

Clusters of blackberry stitches, scattered across a background of easy single crochet, give this classic ripple its unique puffed diamond pattern. The warm throw works up quickly using two strands of yarn held together, and the subdued earth-tone color gives it an air of quiet reserve.

Finished Size: Approximately 45" x 65"

MATERIALS
Worsted Weight Yarn, approximately:
   63 ounces, (1,790 grams, 4,140 yards)
Crochet hook, size N (9.00 mm) **or** size needed for
   gauge

Note: Entire Afghan is worked holding two strands of
   yarn together.

GAUGE: In pattern, 10 sc = 4" and 16 rows = 8½"
         (5" point to point)

PATTERN STITCHES
BEGINNING DECREASE
Pull up a loop in first 2 sts, YO and draw through all
3 loops on hook.
END DECREASE
Pull up a loop in last 2 sts, YO and draw through all 3 loops
on hook.
BLACKBERRY STITCH *(abbreviated BB)*
Insert hook in sc indicated, YO and pull up a loop, (YO
and draw through one loop on hook) 4 times forming a
ch-4 loop, YO and draw through both loops on hook.
Note: Keep ch-4 loop on **right** side of work.

Ch 152 **loosely.**
Row 1 (Right side): Sc in second ch from hook and in
next 6 chs, 3 sc in next ch, sc in next 7 chs, ★ skip next
2 chs, sc in next 7 chs, 3 sc in next ch, sc in next 7 chs;
repeat from ★ across: 153 sc.
Note: Loop a short piece of yarn around any stitch to mark
last row as **right** side.

Rows 2-7: Ch 1, turn; working in Back Loops Only
(Fig. 26, page 124), work beginning decrease, sc in next
6 sc, 3 sc in next sc, ★ sc in next 7 sc, skip next 2 sc, sc in
next 7 sc, 3 sc in next sc; repeat from ★ 7 times **more**, sc
in next 6 sc, work end decrease: 153 sts.
Row 8: Ch 1, turn; working in both loops, work beginning
decrease, sc in next 6 sts, 3 sc in next sc, ★ sc in next 7 sts,
skip next 2 sc, sc in next 7 sts, 3 sc in next sc; repeat from
★ 7 times **more**, sc in next 6 sts, work end decrease.
Row 9: Ch 1, turn; work beginning decrease, sc in next
6 sc, work (BB, sc, BB) in next sc, ★ sc in next 7 sc, skip
next 2 sc, sc in next 7 sc, work (BB, sc, BB) in next sc;
repeat from ★ 7 times **more**, sc in next 6 sc, work end
decrease: 18 BB.
Row 10: Ch 1, turn; work beginning decrease, sc in next
6 sts, 3 sc in next sc, ★ sc in next 7 sts, skip next 2 sc, sc in
next 7 sts, 3 sc in next sc; repeat from ★ 7 times **more**, sc
in next 6 sts, work end decrease.
Row 11: Ch 1, turn; work beginning decrease, sc in next
4 sc, BB in next sc, sc in next sc, work (BB, sc, BB) in next
sc, sc in next sc, BB in next sc, ★ sc in next 5 sc, skip next
2 sc, sc in next 5 sc, BB in next sc, sc in next sc, work (BB,
sc, BB) in next sc, sc in next sc, BB in next sc; repeat from
★ 7 times **more**, sc in next 4 sc, work end decrease: 36 BB.
Rows 12-15: Repeat Rows 8-11.
Rows 16 and 17: Ch 1, turn; work beginning decrease, sc
in next 6 sts, 3 sc in next sc, ★ sc in next 7 sts, skip next
2 sc, sc in next 7 sts, 3 sc in next sc; repeat from ★ 7 times
more, sc in next 6 sts, work end decrease.
Rows 18-119: Repeat Rows 2-17, 6 times; then repeat
Rows 2-7 once **more**.
Finish off.

HEATHER LACE

Enjoy a pampered feeling every time you curl up with this richly colored afghan. Worked in a lacy shell pattern with teal heather yarn, the afghan features an elegant fringed border.

Finished Size: Approximately 45" x 64"

MATERIALS
Worsted Weight Yarn, approximately:
45¹/₂ ounces, (1,290 grams, 2,860 yards)
Crochet hook, size K (6.50 mm) **or** size needed for gauge

GAUGE: In pattern, 14 dc = 4"
11 rows = 5¹/₄"

Note: Afghan is worked from side to side.

BODY
Ch 189 **loosely**.
Row 1 (Right side): Dc in fourth ch from hook and in each ch across: 187 sts.
Note: Loop a short piece of yarn around any stitch to mark last row as **right** side.
Row 2: Ch 1, turn; sc in first dc, (tr in next dc, sc in next st) across pushing each tr to **right** side.
Row 3: Ch 3 (**counts as first dc, now and throughout**), turn; (dc in next tr, dc in next sc) across.
Row 4: Ch 4 (**counts as first dc plus ch 1, now and throughout**), turn; skip next dc, dc in next dc, (ch 1, skip next dc, dc in next dc) across: 93 ch-1 sps.
Row 5: Ch 3, turn; (dc in next ch-1 sp, dc in next dc) across: 187 dc.
Rows 6 and 7: Repeat Rows 2 and 3.
Finish off.
Note: To work **Shell**, (2 dc, ch 1, 2 dc) in st or sp indicated.
Row 8: With **right** side facing, join yarn with slip st in first dc; ch 3, 2 dc in same st, ch 2, (skip next 5 dc, work Shell in next dc, ch 2) across to last 6 dc, skip next 5 dc, 3 dc in last dc: 30 Shells.

Row 9: Ch 3, turn; 2 dc in same st, ch 2, ★ work Shell in next Shell (ch-1 sp), ch 2; repeat from ★ across, skip last ch-2 sp and next 2 dc, 3 dc in last dc.
Row 10: Ch 3, turn; 2 dc in same st, ch 1, sc around chs of last 2 rows, ch 1, ★ work Shell in next Shell, ch 1, sc around chs of last 2 rows, ch 1; repeat from ★ across, skip next 2 dc, 3 dc in last dc.
Row 11: Ch 1, turn; sc in first dc, ch 5 **loosely**, (sc in next Shell, ch 5 **loosely**) across, skip next 2 ch-1 sps and next 2 dc, sc in last dc: 31 loops.
Row 12: Ch 3, turn; (dc in next 5 chs, dc in next sc) across: 187 dc.
Row 13: Ch 1, turn; sc in first dc, (tr in next dc, sc in next dc) across pushing each tr to **right** side.
Rows 14-95: Repeat Rows 3-13, 7 times; then repeat Rows 3-7 once **more**.
Finish off.

BORDER
Row 1: With **right** side facing and working in end of rows, join yarn with slip st in first row; ch 3, work 156 dc evenly spaced across: 157 dc.
Rows 2-10: Work same as Body.
Finish off.
Repeat across opposite end; at end of Row 10, do **not** finish off.

EDGING
First Side: Ch 1, sc evenly across end of Border rows, sc in each st across, sc evenly across end of Border rows; finish off.
Second Side: With **right** side facing, join yarn with slip st in end of first Border row on opposite side; work same as First Side.

Add fringe (*Figs. 31a & c, page 126*).

ELEGANT HARMONY

Richly textured popcorn stitches and a classic ripple design combine in graceful harmony for this plush afghan. Worked holding two strands of soft green yarn together, the stylish throw is a true gem to crochet.

Finished Size: Approximately 48" x 66"

MATERIALS
Worsted Weight Yarn, approximately:
  70 ounces, (1,990 grams, 4,600 yards)
  Crochet hook, size N (9.00 mm) **or** size needed for gauge

Note: Entire Afghan is worked holding two strands of yarn together.

GAUGE: In pattern, 10 dc = 4" and 4 rows = 4¹/2"
      (8" point to point)

PATTERN STITCHES
CENTER DECREASE (uses next 5 sts or sps)
★ YO, insert hook in **next** st or sp, YO and pull up a loop, YO and draw through 2 loops on hook; repeat from ★ 4 times **more**, YO and draw through all 6 loops on hook.
DECREASE (uses next 3 sts or sps)
★ YO, insert hook in **next** st or sp, YO and pull up a loop, YO and draw through 2 loops on hook; repeat from ★ 2 times **more**, YO and draw through all 4 loops on hook.
POPCORN
5 Dc in st indicated, drop loop from hook, insert hook in first dc of 5-dc group, hook dropped loop and draw through **(Fig. 9a, page 119)**.

Ch 149 **loosely**.
Row 1: YO, insert hook in fourth ch from hook, YO and pull up a loop, YO and draw through 2 loops on hook, (YO, insert hook in **next** ch, YO and pull up a loop, YO and draw through 2 loops on hook) twice, YO and draw through all 4 loops on hook, dc in next 9 chs, 5 dc in next ch, dc in next 9 chs, ★ work center decrease, dc in next 9 chs, 5 dc in next ch, dc in next 9 chs; repeat from ★ across to last 4 chs, decrease, dc in last ch: 147 sts.

Row 2 (Right side): Ch 3 **(counts as first dc, now and throughout)**, turn; working in Back Loops Only **(Fig. 26, page 124)**, decrease, ch 1, (skip next dc, dc in next dc, ch 1) 4 times, skip next dc, 5 dc in next dc, ch 1, (skip next dc, dc in next dc, ch 1) 4 times, ★ skip next dc, work center decrease, ch 1, (skip next dc, dc in next dc, ch 1) 4 times, skip next dc, 5 dc in next dc, ch 1, (skip next dc, dc in next dc, ch 1) 4 times; repeat from ★ across to last 5 sts, skip next dc, decrease, dc in top of beginning ch: 6 5-dc groups.
Row 3: Ch 3, turn; working in both loops of each dc and in each sp, decrease, dc in next ch-1 sp, (dc in next dc, dc in next ch-1 sp) 3 times, dc in next 2 dc, 5 dc in next dc, dc in next 2 dc, dc in next ch-1 sp, (dc in next dc, dc in next ch-1 sp) 3 times, ★ work center decrease, dc in next ch-1 sp, (dc in next dc, dc in next ch-1 sp) 3 times, dc in next 2 dc, 5 dc in next dc, dc in next 2 dc, dc in next ch-1 sp, (dc in next dc, dc in next ch-1 sp) 3 times; repeat from ★ across to last 4 sts, decrease, dc in last dc: 147 sts.
Row 4: Ch 3, turn; working in Back Loops Only, decrease, ch 1, (skip next dc, work Popcorn in next dc, ch 2) 4 times, skip next dc, work (Popcorn, ch 3, Popcorn) in next dc, ch 2, (skip next dc, work Popcorn in next dc, ch 2) 4 times, ★ skip next dc, work center decrease, ch 1, (skip next dc, work Popcorn in next dc, ch 2) 4 times, skip next dc, work (Popcorn, ch 3, Popcorn) in next dc, ch 2, (skip next dc, work Popcorn in next dc, ch 2) 4 times; repeat from ★ across to last 5 sts, skip next dc, decrease, dc in last dc: 60 Popcorns.
Row 5: Ch 3, turn; working in both loops of each Popcorn and in each sp, decrease, (dc in next sp, dc in next Popcorn) 4 times, 7 dc in next sp, (dc in next Popcorn, dc in next sp) 4 times, ★ work center decrease, (dc in next sp, dc in next Popcorn) 4 times, 7 dc in next sp, (dc in next Popcorn, dc in next sp) 4 times; repeat from ★ across to last 4 sts, decrease, dc in last dc: 6 7-dc groups.
Repeat Rows 2-5 until Afghan measures approximately 66", ending by working Row 3.
Finish off.

DISTINCTIVE DESIGN

Fashioned in subtly shaded strips of peach and cream, this mile-a-minute afghan is quick to crochet using basic stitches. The textured panels are joined with a simple combination of slip stitches and chains to create the distinctive scalloped borders.

Finished Size: Approximately 50" x 69"

MATERIALS

Worsted Weight Yarn, approximately:
Color A (Peach) - 20 ounces,
(570 grams, 1,315 yards)
Color B (Off-White) - 17 ounces,
(480 grams, 1,120 yards)
Color C (Dark Peach) - 6 ounces,
(170 grams, 395 yards)
Crochet hook, size K (6.50 mm) **or** size needed for gauge
Yarn needle

GAUGE: 12 sc and 14 rows = 4"
One Strip = 5¹/₂" wide

STRIP (Make 9)

With Color C, ch 198 **loosely**.

Foundation Row (Wrong side)**:** Sc in second ch from hook, (tr in next ch, sc in next ch) across; finish off: 197 sts.

Note: Loop a short piece of yarn around **first** sc to mark last row as **wrong** side and bottom edge.

Rnd 1: With **right** side facing, join Color A with slip st in end of Foundation Row at top edge; ch 4 **(counts as first dc plus ch 1, now and throughout)**, (dc, ch 1) 7 times in same row, skip first sc and next tr, dc in next sc, ch 1, (skip next tr, dc in next sc, ch 1) across to last 2 sts, skip last 2 sts, (dc, ch 1) 8 times in end of Foundation Row at bottom edge; working in free loops of beginning ch *(Fig. 27b, page 124)*, skip first 2 chs, dc in next ch, ch 1, (skip next ch, dc in next ch, ch 1) 96 times, skip next 2 chs; join with slip st to first dc, finish off: 210 dc.

Rnd 2: With **wrong** side facing, join Color B with slip st in same st as joining; ch 1, sc in same st, tr in next ch-1 sp, (sc in next dc, tr in next ch-1 sp) around; join with slip st to first sc, finish off: 420 sts.

Note: To work **V-St**, (dc, ch 1, dc) in next sc.

Rnd 3: With **right** side facing, join Color A with slip st in same st as joining; ch 4, skip next tr, dc in next sc, ch 1, skip next tr, (work V-St, ch 1, skip next tr) 4 times, (dc in next sc, ch 1, skip next tr) 101 times, (work V-St, ch 1, skip next tr) 4 times, (dc in next sc, ch 1, skip next tr) across; join with slip st to first dc, do **not** finish off: 202 dc and 8 V-Sts.

Rnd 4: Ch 1, turn; sc in same st, tr in next ch-1 sp, (sc in next dc, tr in next ch-1 sp) around; join with slip st to first sc, finish off: 436 sts.

Rnd 5: With **right** side facing, join Color B with slip st in same st as joining; ch 4, skip next tr, (dc in next sc, ch 1, skip next tr) twice, (work V-St, ch 1, skip next tr) 5 times, place marker around last ch-1 made for joining placement, (dc in next sc, ch 1, skip next tr) 104 times, (work V-St, ch 1, skip next tr) 5 times, (dc in next sc, ch 1, skip next tr) across; join with slip st to first dc, finish off: 208 dc and 10 V-Sts.

ASSEMBLY

With **wrong** side of two Strips together, bottom edges at same end and working through both loops of both pieces, join Color B with slip st in marked ch-1 sp; (ch 2, skip next dc, slip st in next ch-1 sp) across to next V-St; finish off. Join remaining Strips in same manner, always working in the same direction.

EDGING

With **right** side facing, join Color B with slip st in any ch-1 sp; (ch 2, slip st in next ch-1 sp) around; join with slip st to first slip st, finish off.

FILET DIAMONDS

Diamonds are forever, and this pretty afghan has timeless appeal! Easy to make by joining panels of filet crochet, the simple throw is guaranteed to add sparkle to your home.

Finished Size: Approximately 47" x 69"

MATERIALS
Worsted Weight Yarn, approximately:
38½ ounces, (1,090 grams, 2,530 yards)
Crochet hook, size H (5.00 mm) **or** size needed for gauge

GAUGE: 23 sts and 12 rows = 6"

PANEL (Make 7)

Ch 25 **loosely**.

Row 1 (Right side): Dc in fourth ch from hook and in next 9 chs, ch 1, skip next ch, dc in last 11 chs: 23 sts.

Note: Loop a short piece of yarn around any stitch to mark last row as **right** side and bottom edge.

Row 2: Ch 3 **(counts as first dc, now and throughout)**, turn; dc in next 8 dc, ch 1, skip next dc, dc in next dc and in next ch-1 sp, dc in next dc, ch 1, skip next dc, dc in last 9 dc.

Row 3: Ch 3, turn; dc in next 6 dc, ch 1, skip next dc, dc in next dc and in next ch-1 sp, dc in next 3 dc, dc in next ch-1 sp and in next dc, ch 1, skip next dc, dc in last 7 dc.

Row 4: Ch 3, turn; dc in next 4 dc, ch 1, skip next dc, dc in next dc and in next ch-1 sp, dc in next 7 dc, dc in next ch-1 sp and in next dc, ch 1, skip next dc, dc in last 5 dc.

Row 5: Ch 3, turn; dc in next 2 dc, ch 1, skip next dc, dc in next dc and next ch-1 sp, dc in next 11 dc, dc in next ch-1 sp and in next dc, ch 1, skip next dc, dc in last 3 dc.

Row 6: Ch 3, turn; dc in next 2 dc, dc in next ch-1 sp and in next dc, ch 1, skip next dc, dc in next 11 dc, ch 1, skip next dc, dc in next dc and in next ch-1 sp, dc in last 3 dc.

Row 7: Ch 3, turn; dc in next 4 dc, dc in next ch-1 sp and in next dc, ch 1, skip next dc, dc in next 7 dc, ch 1, skip next dc, dc in next dc and in next ch-1 sp, dc in last 5 dc.

Row 8: Ch 3, turn; dc in next 6 dc, dc in next ch-1 sp and in next dc, ch 1, skip next dc, dc in next 3 dc, ch 1, skip next dc, dc in next dc and in next ch-1 sp, dc in last 7 dc.

Row 9: Ch 3, turn; dc in next 8 dc, dc in next ch-1 sp and in next dc, ch 1, skip next dc, dc in next dc and in next ch-1 sp, dc in last 9 dc.

Rows 10-137: Repeat Rows 2-9, 16 times.
Finish off.

ASSEMBLY

With **wrong** side of two Panels together, bottom edges at the same end and working in end of rows, join yarn with slip st in corner of **first** Panel; ch 2, sc in corner of **second** Panel, ch 2, sc in first row on **first** Panel, ch 2, sc in top of first dc on **second** Panel, ch 2, (sc in next row on **first** Panel, ch 2, sc in top of next dc on **second** Panel, ch 2) across, slip st in corner of **first** Panel; finish off.
Join remaining Panels in same manner, always working in the same direction.

EDGING

Rnd 1: With **right** side facing, join yarn with slip st in any dc; ch 1, sc evenly around working 3 sc in each corner; join with slip st to first sc.

Rnd 2: Ch 1, sc in each sc around working 3 sc in each corner; join with slip st to first sc, finish off.

LACY SHELLS

*This lacy throw is simply elegant, and it's extra-easy to crochet, too.
The delicate shell pattern is created using only two basic stitches —
chain and double crochet. It's a lovely accent for any room!*

Finished Size: Approximately 48" x 65"

MATERIALS
Worsted Weight Yarn, approximately:
39 ounces, (1,110 grams, 2,485 yards)
Crochet hook, size N (9.00 mm) **or** size needed for
gauge

GAUGE: 3 Shells and 5 rows = 4"

Note: To work **Shell**, (3 dc, ch 1, dc) in st or sp indicated.

Ch 133 **loosely**.
Row 1 (Right side): Work Shell in sixth ch from hook,
★ skip next 3 chs, work Shell in next ch; repeat from ★
across to last 3 chs, skip next 2 chs, dc in last ch: 32 Shells.
Note: Loop a short piece of yarn around any stitch to mark
last row as **right** side.
Row 2: Ch 3 **(counts as first dc, now and throughout)**,
turn; work Shell in ch-1 sp of each Shell across, dc in top
of beginning ch: 32 Shells.
Row 3: Ch 3, turn; work Shell in ch-1 sp of each Shell
across, dc in last dc.
Repeat Row 3 until Afghan measures approximately 63",
ending by working a **right** side row; do **not** finish off.

EDGING
Rnd 1: Ch 1, do **not** turn; 3 sc in corner, work 2 sc in end
of each row across to next corner; 3 sc in corner, work
128 sc evenly spaced across beginning ch to next corner;
3 sc in corner, work 2 sc in end of each row across to next
corner; 3 sc in corner, work 128 sc evenly spaced across sts
of last row; join with slip st to first sc.
Rnd 2: Ch 1, sc in same st, ch 3, skip next sc, (sc in next
sc, ch 3, skip next sc) around; join with slip st to first sc.
Rnd 3: (Slip st, ch 2, dc) in first ch-3 sp and in each
ch-3 sp around; join with slip st to first slip st, finish off.

TIMELESS FLOWERS

This romantic afghan forever preserves the timeless beauty of flowers. Luxuriously plush because it's worked holding two strands of yarn together, the wrap features a delicate scalloped border and motifs that resemble rosy blossoms. The "blooms" are worked separately and then slip stitched together, making this feminine throw an easy choice for beginners.

Finished Size: Approximately 46" x 58"

MATERIALS
Worsted Weight Yarn, approximately:
MC (Ecru) - 31 ounces, (880 grams, 1,950 yards)
Color A (Rose) - 12 ounces, (340 grams, 755 yards)
Color B (Green) - 16 ounces,
(450 grams, 1,005 yards)
Crochet hook, size N (9.00 mm) **or** size needed for gauge

Note: Entire Afghan is worked holding two strands of yarn together.

GAUGE: One Motif = 6"

MOTIF (Make 63)
With Color A, ch 5; join with slip st to form a ring.
Rnd 1 (Right side): Ch 1, (sc in ring, ch 7) 8 times; join with slip st to first sc, finish off: 8 loops.
Note: Loop a short piece of yarn around any stitch to mark last round as **right** side.
Rnd 2: With **wrong** side facing, join Color B with slip st in any loop; ch 1, sc in same loop, (3 dc, ch 2, 3 dc) in next loop, ★ sc in next loop, (3 dc, ch 2, 3 dc) in next loop; repeat from ★ around; join with slip st to first sc, finish off.
Rnd 3: With **right** side facing, join MC with slip st in any ch-2 sp; ch 3, (dc, tr, 2 dc) in same sp, dc in next 7 sts, ★ (2 dc, tr, 2 dc) in next ch-2 sp, dc in next 7 sts; repeat from ★ around; join with slip st to top of beginning ch-3, finish off: 48 sts.

ASSEMBLY
Afghan is assembled by joining Motifs together, forming 7 vertical strips of 9 Motifs each and then by joining strips. Join Motifs as follows: With **right** sides together and working through outside loops, join MC with slip st in corner tr; slip st in each st across to next corner tr; finish off.
Join strips in same manner.

EDGING
Rnd 1: With **right** side facing, join MC with slip st in any corner tr; ch 1, 3 sc in same st, ★ sc in each st across to next corner tr, 3 sc in corner tr; repeat from ★ 2 times **more**, sc in each st across; join with slip st to first sc.
Rnd 2: Ch 1, sc in same st, ch 3, skip next sc, ★ sc in next sc, ch 3, skip next sc; repeat from ★ around; join with slip st to first sc, finish off.

SOFT AND SWEET

A harmony of dreamy pastels and lacy patterns, the pretty afghans in this delicate collection offer a gentle touch for the boudoir or nursery. The feathery softness of our baby afghans will give a warm welcome to the newest member of the family. Or you can choose one of our full-size throws to bring a decidedly feminine flair to your bedroom or sitting room. Easy to crochet with our quick techniques, these sweet wraps will enfold you with tenderness.

ROSE RHAPSODY

Decidedly feminine, this mile-a-minute afghan is poetry in motion. Created in strips of rose and ecru using a unique overlay technique, its pretty pattern will add elegance to any boudoir.

Finished Size: Approximately 54" x 72"

MATERIALS
Worsted Weight Yarn, approximately:
MC (Rose) - 41 ounces, (1,160 grams, 2,695 yards)
CC (Ecru) - 20½ ounces, (580 grams, 1,345 yards)
Crochet hook, size K (6.50 mm) **or** size needed for gauge
Yarn needle

GAUGE: 15 dc and 7 rows = 4"
One Strip = 3½" wide

STRIP (Make 15)
CENTER
With MC, ch 265 **loosely**.
Row 1 (Right side): Dc in fourth ch from hook and in each ch across: 263 sts.
Note: Loop a short piece of yarn around any stitch to mark last row as **right** side.
Rows 2 and 3: Ch 3 **(counts as first dc, now and throughout)**, turn; dc in next st and in each st across. Finish off.

OVERLAY
Note: To work **Front Post treble crochet** *(abbreviated FPtr)*, YO twice, insert hook from **front** to **back** around post of dc indicated, YO and pull up a loop (4 loops on hook) *(Fig. 12, page 119)*, (YO and draw through 2 loops on hook) 3 times.
FIRST SIDE
With **right** side facing and working in sts of Row 3, join CC with slip st in first dc; ch 1, sc in same st and in next dc, work 3 FPtr around fourth dc on Row 2, ★ skip next 3 dc, sc in next dc, skip next 3 dc on Row 2 and work 3 FPtr around next dc; repeat from ★ across to last 5 dc, skip next 3 dc, sc in last 2 dc; finish off: 263 sts.

SECOND SIDE
With **right** side facing and working in free loops of beginning ch *(Fig. 27b, page 124)*, join CC with slip st in first ch; ch 1, sc in same ch and in next ch, work 3 FPtr around post of fourth dc on Row 2 (same dc as First Side), ★ skip next 3 chs, sc in next ch, skip next 3 dc on Row 2 and work 3 FPtr around post of next dc; repeat from ★ across to last 7 chs, skip next 3 chs, sc in next 2 chs, leave remaining 2 chs unworked; finish off: 263 sts.

EDGING
FIRST SIDE
With **right** side facing, join MC with slip st in Back Loop Only of first sc *(Fig. 26, page 124)*; ch 3, dc in Back Loop Only of next st and in each st across; finish off: 263 dc.

SECOND SIDE
Work same as First Side.

ASSEMBLY
With **wrong** side of two Strips together and using MC, whipstitch Strips together working in inside loops *(Fig. 29a, page 125)*.
Join remaining Strips in same manner, always working from the same direction.

BORDER
With **right** side of long edge facing, join CC with slip st in first dc; ch 1, sc in same st, † (ch 2, skip next dc, sc in next dc) across; working in end of rows, 2 dc in first row, skip next row (CC row), 3 tr in each of next 3 rows, skip next row (CC row), 2 dc in next row, ★ sc in joining, 2 dc in next row, skip next row (CC row), 3 tr in each of next 3 rows, skip next row (CC row), 2 dc in next row; repeat from ★ across to corner †, sc in first dc, repeat from † to † once; join with slip st to first sc, finish off.

WHITE LACE

A combination of clusters and front post treble crochet stitches gives this afghan its fancy openwork look. For feathery softness, we fashioned the lacy throw using brushed acrylic yarn and then added a long, flowing fringe.

Finished Size: Approximately 49" x 68"

MATERIALS
Worsted Weight Brushed Acrylic Yarn, approximately:
     49 ounces, (1,390 grams, 3,780 yards)
Crochet hook, size H (5.00 mm) **or** size needed for gauge

GAUGE: In pattern, 14 sts and 11 rows = 4"
    Gauge Swatch: (3³/4" x 4")
    Ch 15 **loosely**.
    Work same as Afghan for 11 rows.
    Finish off.

PATTERN STITCHES
FRONT POST TREBLE CROCHET
(abbreviated FPtr)
YO twice, insert hook from **front** to **back** around post of st indicated, YO and pull up a loop (4 loops on hook) *(Fig. 12, page 119)*, (YO and draw through 2 loops on hook) 3 times.
BEGINNING CLUSTER (uses first 2 dc)
Ch 2, turn; YO, insert hook in **next** dc, YO and pull up a loop, (YO and draw through 2 loops on hook) twice.
CLUSTER (uses next 3 dc)
★ YO, insert hook in **next** dc, YO and pull up loop, YO and draw through 2 loops on hook; repeat from ★ 2 times **more**, YO and draw through all 4 loops on hook.
END CLUSTER (uses last 2 dc)
★ YO, insert hook in **next** dc, YO and pull up loop, YO and draw through 2 loops on hook; repeat from ★ once **more**, YO and draw through all 3 loops on hook.

Ch 171 **loosely**.
Row 1 (Right side): Dc in fourth ch from hook and in each ch across: 169 sts.
Note: Loop a short piece of yarn around any stitch to mark last row as **right** side.

Row 2: Ch 1, turn; sc in each st across: 169 sc.
Row 3: Ch 3 **(counts as first dc, now and throughout)**, turn; dc in next sc and in each sc across.
Row 4: Ch 1, turn; sc in each dc across.
Row 5: Ch 1, turn; sc in first sc, ★ work FPtr around dc one row **below** next sc, skip sc behind FPtr, sc in next sc; repeat from ★ across: 84 FPtr.
Row 6: Ch 1, turn; sc in each st across: 169 sc.
Row 7: Ch 1, turn; sc in first sc, ★ work FPtr around FPtr one row **below** next sc, skip sc behind FPtr, sc in next sc; repeat from ★ across: 84 FPtr.
Row 8: Ch 1, turn; sc in each st across: 169 sc.
Row 9: Ch 3, turn; dc in next sc and in each sc across.
Row 10: Ch 1, turn; sc in each dc across.
Row 11: Ch 3, turn; dc in same st, (skip next 2 sc, 3 dc in next sc) across to last 3 sc, skip next 2 sc, 2 dc in last sc.
Row 12: Work beginning Cluster, ch 2, (work Cluster, ch 2) across to last 2 dc, work end Cluster: 57 Clusters.
Row 13: Ch 1, turn; sc in first Cluster, (2 sc in next ch-2 sp, sc in next Cluster) across: 169 sc.
Row 14: Ch 1, turn; sc in each sc across.
Rows 15-22: Repeat Rows 11-14 twice.
Row 23: Ch 3, turn; dc in next sc and in each sc across.
Repeat Rows 2-23 until Afghan measures approximately 67", ending by working Row 9.
Finish off.

EDGING
FIRST END
With **right** side facing and working across last row, join yarn with slip st in first dc; ch 1, sc in same st, ★ ch 3, skip next dc, sc in next dc; repeat from ★ across; finish off.

SECOND END
With **right** side facing and working in free loops of beginning ch *(Fig. 27b, page 124)*, join yarn with slip st in first ch; ch 1, sc in same st, ★ ch 3, skip next ch, sc in next ch; repeat from ★ across; finish off.

Add fringe in each ch-3 sp across both ends *(Figs. 31a & c, page 126)*.

KEEPSAKE COVER-UP

Featuring soft shells and a pretty scalloped border, this precious cover-up is just right for a trip to Grandma's house. It's quicker to finish than most baby afghans because you use worsted weight yarn, and its classic style will make it a favorite for generations!

Finished Size: Approximately 32" x 45"

MATERIALS
Worsted Weight Brushed Acrylic Yarn, approximately:
    14 ounces, (400 grams, 1,080 yards)
Crochet hook, size K (6.50 mm) **or** size needed for gauge

GAUGE: In pattern, 19 stitches (2 repeats) and 8 rows = 5³/₄"
    Gauge Swatch: (5³/₄" x 5³/₄")
    Ch 22 **loosely.**
    Work same as Afghan for 8 rows.
    Finish off.

Ch 102 **loosely.**

Row 1: Dc in sixth ch from hook, ★ skip next 2 chs, 5 dc in next ch, skip next 2 chs, dc in next ch, ch 1, skip next ch, dc in next ch; repeat from ★ across: 12 5-dc groups.

Row 2: Ch 4 (**counts as first dc plus ch 1, now and throughout**), turn; ★ dc in next dc, skip next 2 dc, 5 dc in next dc, skip next 2 dc, dc in next dc, ch 1; repeat from ★ 11 times **more**, skip next ch, dc in next ch.

Row 3: Ch 4, turn; dc in next dc, ★ skip next 2 dc, 5 dc in next dc, skip next 2 dc, dc in next dc, ch 1, dc in next dc; repeat from ★ across.

Repeat Row 3 until Afghan measures approximately 42", do **not** finish off.

EDGING

Rnd 1 (Right side)**:** Ch 3, turn; 2 dc in same st, work 93 dc evenly spaced across to last dc, 3 dc in last dc; work 117 dc evenly spaced across end of rows; working in free loops of beginning ch (**Fig. 27b, page 124**), 3 dc in first ch, work 93 dc evenly spaced across to last ch, 3 dc in last ch; work 117 dc evenly spaced across end of rows; join with slip st to top of beginning ch-3: 432 sts.

Rnd 2: Slip st in next dc, ch 3, 4 dc in same st, skip next 2 dc, sc in next dc, skip next 2 dc, ★ 5 dc in next dc, skip next 2 dc, sc in next dc, skip next 2 dc; repeat from ★ around; join with slip st to top of beginning ch-3, finish off.

ROSEBUDS

The pretty three-dimensional buds on this afghan conjure up images of richly colored roses on a delicate trellis. Super-quick to make, the flowery throw is worked in double crochet stitches while holding three strands of yarn together. An edging of green and rose completes the lovely look.

Finished Size: Approximately 46" x 62"

MATERIALS
Worsted Weight Yarn, approximately:
MC (Ecru) - 42 ounces, (1,190 grams, 2,625 yards)
Color A (Rose) - 4 ounces, (110 grams, 250 yards)
Color B (Green) - 2 ounces, (60 grams, 125 yards)
Crochet hook, size Q (15.00 mm) **or** size needed for gauge
Yarn needle

Note: Entire Afghan is worked holding three strands of yarn together, unless otherwise specified.

GAUGE: 7 dc = 6" and 5 rows = 6½"

With MC, ch 52 **loosely.**
Row 1: Dc in sixth ch from hook, ★ ch 1, skip next ch, dc in next ch; repeat from ★ across: 24 sps.
Row 2 (Right side): Ch 4 **(counts as first dc plus ch 1, now and throughout),** turn; dc in next dc, (dc in next ch-1 sp, dc in next dc) across to last sp, ch 1, skip next ch, dc in next ch: 47 dc.
Note: Loop a short piece of yarn around any stitch to mark last row as **right** side.
Row 3: Ch 4, turn; dc in next dc and in each dc across to last dc, ch 1, dc in last dc.
Row 4: Ch 4, turn; dc in next 4 dc, dc in Back Loop Only of next dc *(Fig. 26, page 124)*, (dc in **both** loops of next 11 dc, dc in Back Loop Only of next dc) 3 times, dc in **both** loops of next 4 dc, ch 1, dc in last dc.
Rows 5-7: Ch 4, turn; dc in next dc and in each dc across to last dc, ch 1, dc in last dc.
Row 8: Ch 4, turn; dc in next 10 dc, dc in Back Loop Only of next dc, (dc in **both** loops of next 11 dc, dc in Back Loop Only of next dc) twice, dc in **both** loops of next 10 dc, ch 1, dc in last dc.
Rows 9-11: Ch 4, turn; dc in next dc and in each dc across to last dc, ch 1, dc in last dc.

Repeat Rows 4-11 until Afghan measures approximately 57", ending by working Row 6.
Last Row: Ch 4, turn; dc in next dc, ★ ch 1, skip next dc, dc in next dc; repeat from ★ across to last dc, ch 1, dc in last dc; do **not** finish off: 24 sps.

EDGING
Rnd 1: Ch 3, turn; 2 dc in first sp and in each sp across to next corner sp, (5 dc in corner sp, 2 dc in each sp across to next corner sp) around, 2 dc in same sp as beginning ch; join with slip st to top of beginning ch-3, finish off.
Rnd 2: With **right** side facing and using 2 strands of Color A held together, join Color A with slip st in same st as joining; ch 1, sc in same st and in each dc around; join with slip st to first sc, finish off.
Trim: With **right** side facing and using one strand of Color B, join Color B with slip st around post of beginning ch-3 on Rnd 1 *(Fig. 10, page 119)*; ch 1, sc **loosely** around post of same st and around post of each dc around; join with slip st to first sc, finish off.

ROSEBUD
With **right** side facing and using 2 strands of Color A held together, join Color A with slip st in any free loop on Row 3 *(Fig. 27a, page 124)*; ch 3, 2 dc in same st, drop loop from hook, insert hook in top of beginning ch-3, hook dropped loop and draw through; finish off leaving an 8" length for sewing.
Sew top of Rosebud at an angle to top of next row.
Work a Rosebud in each remaining free loop.

STEM
Cut a 12" length of Color B and fold in half. With **right** side facing, insert hook around base of Rosebud; draw folded end through and pull loose ends through folded end. Tighten slightly and trim ends.
Repeat around each Rosebud.

ROCK-A-BYE WRAP

With this pretty mile-a-minute wrap, rocking your little one to sleep will be extra special. Created in soft green and white, it features a pretty pattern of clusters worked around a simple foundation row. The lacy afghan offers baby a cozy place to snuggle up and nap — for those quiet moments a new mother will always treasure.

Finished Size: Approximately 36" x 45"

MATERIALS
Sport Weight Yarn, approximately:
  MC (Green) - 8¹/4 ounces, (230 grams, 825 yards)
  CC (White) - 3¹/2 ounces, (100 grams, 350 yards)
Crochet hook, size H (5.00 mm) **or** size needed for gauge

GAUGE: 16 dc and 8 rows = 4"
  One Strip = 4" wide

FIRST STRIP
With CC, ch 165 **loosely**.
Foundation Row (Right side): Hdc in fifth ch from hook, ★ ch 1, skip next ch, hdc in next ch; repeat from ★ across: 81 sps.
Note: Loop a short piece of yarn around any stitch to mark last row as **right** side.
Rnd 1: Ch 1, in end sp work (sc, ch 1, dc, ch 1, sc, ch 1, 2 dc, ch 1, sc), ch 1; working in free loops of beginning ch *(Fig. 27b, page 124)*, dc in next 3 chs, ch 1, (sc in next ch, ch 1, dc in next 3 chs, ch 1) across to last sp, in last sp work (sc, ch 1, 2 dc, ch 1, sc, ch 1, dc, ch 1, sc, ch 1, 2 dc, ch 1, sc), ch 1; working in sts across Foundation Row, dc in next 3 sts, ch 1, (sc in next st, ch 1, dc in next 3 sts, ch 1) across, (sc, ch 1, 2 dc) in same end sp as first sc, ch 1; join with slip st to first sc, finish off: 80 3-dc groups.
Rnd 2: With **right** side facing, join MC with slip st in center dc on either end; ch 3, 3 dc in same st, 4 dc in each of next 2 dc, 4 dc in center dc of each 3-dc group across, 4 dc in each of next 5 dc, 4 dc in center dc of each 3-dc group across, 4 dc in each of next 2 dc; join with slip st to top of beginning ch-3, do **not** finish off: 90 4-dc groups.

Note #1: To work **beginning Cluster** (uses next 3 sts), ch 2 ★ YO, insert hook in **next** dc, YO and pull up a loop, YO and draw through 2 loops on hook; repeat from ★ 2 times **more**, YO and draw through all 4 loops on hook.
Note #2: To work **Cluster** (uses next 4 dc), ★ YO, insert hook in **next** dc, YO and pull up a loop, YO and draw through 2 loops on hook; repeat from ★ 3 times **more**, YO and draw through all 5 loops on hook.
Rnd 3: Work beginning Cluster, ch 6, work Cluster, ch 6, (work Cluster, ch 4) 41 times, (work Cluster, ch 6) 4 times, (work Cluster, ch 4) 41 times, (work Cluster, ch 6) twice; join with slip st to top of beginning Cluster: 90 Clusters.
Rnd 4: Ch 3, [(slip st, ch 1) 3 times in next loop, slip st in next Cluster, ch 3] twice, [(slip st, ch 1) twice in next loop, slip st in next Cluster, ch 3] 41 times, [(slip st, ch 1) 3 times in next loop, slip st in next Cluster, ch 3] 4 times, [(slip st, ch 1) twice in next loop, slip st in next Cluster, ch 3] 41 times, (slip st, ch 1) 3 times in next loop, slip st in next Cluster, ch 3, (slip st, ch 1) 3 times in last loop; join with slip st at base of beginning ch-3, finish off.

REMAINING 8 STRIPS
Work same as First Strip through Rnd 3: 90 Clusters.
Rnd 4 (Joining rnd): Ch 3, [(slip st, ch 1) 3 times in next loop, slip st in next Cluster, ch 3] twice, [(slip st, ch 1) twice in next loop, slip st in next Cluster, ch 3] 41 times, [(slip st, ch 1) 3 times in next loop, slip st in next Cluster, ch 3] 3 times, (slip st, ch 1) 3 times in next loop, slip st in next Cluster, ch 1, place Strips with **wrong** sides together, slip st in corresponding ch-3 sp on **previous** Strip, ch 1, ★ (slip st, ch 1) twice in next loop on **new** Strip, slip st in next Cluster, ch 1, slip st in next ch-3 sp on **previous** Strip, ch 1; repeat from ★ 40 times **more**, (slip st, ch 1) 3 times in next loop, slip st in next Cluster, ch 3, (slip st, ch 1) 3 times in last loop; join with slip st at base of beginning ch-3, finish off.

VINTAGE RIPPLE

This luxurious throw will bring the elegance of yesteryear to any room. Worked in half double crochet stitches using two strands of yarn, the classic ripple afghan features openwork rows of puff stitches for timeless appeal.

Finished Size: Approximately 56" x 74"

MATERIALS
Worsted Weight Yarn, approximately:
66 ounces, (1,870 grams, 4,340 yards)
Crochet hook, size N (9.00 mm) **or** size needed for gauge

Note: Entire Afghan is worked holding two strands of yarn together.

GAUGE: In pattern, 9 hdc and 6 rows = 4¹/₂"
(9¹/₄" point to point)

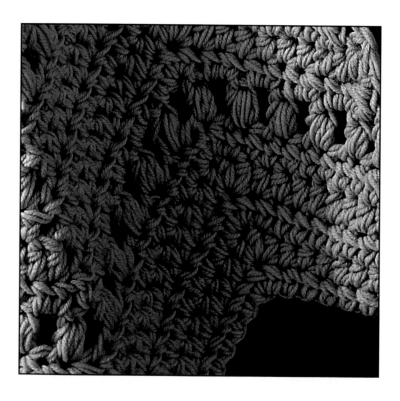

Ch 137 **loosely.**

Row 1 (Right side): Hdc in third ch from hook and in next 8 chs, 3 hdc in next ch, hdc in next 10 chs, ★ skip next 2 chs, hdc in next 10 chs, 3 hdc in next ch, hdc in next 10 chs; repeat from ★ across: 138 sts.

Note: Loop a short piece of yarn around any stitch to mark last row as **right** side.

Rows 2-5: Ch 2 (**counts as first hdc, now and throughout**), turn; (YO, insert hook in **next** st, YO and pull up a loop) twice, YO and draw through all 5 loops on hook, hdc in next 8 hdc, 3 hdc in next hdc, ★ hdc in next 10 hdc, skip next 2 hdc, hdc in next 10 hdc, 3 hdc in next hdc; repeat from ★ across to last 11 sts, hdc in next 8 hdc, (YO, insert hook in **next** hdc, YO and pull up a loop) twice, YO and draw through all 5 loops on hook, hdc in last st.

Note: To work **Puff St,** (YO, insert hook in hdc indicated, YO and pull up a loop even with last st worked) 3 times, YO and draw through all 7 loops on hook (**Fig. 22, page 122**).

Row 6: Ch 2, turn; work Puff St in next st, (ch 2, skip next st, work Puff St in next st) 10 times, ★ ch 1, skip next 2 sts, work Puff St in next st, (ch 2, skip next st, work Puff St in next st) 10 times; repeat from ★ across to last st, hdc in last hdc: 66 Puff Sts.

Row 7: Ch 2, turn; YO, insert hook in first Puff St, YO and pull up a loop, YO, insert hook in next ch-2 sp, YO and pull up a loop, YO and draw through all 5 loops on hook, (hdc in next Puff St and in next ch-2 sp) 4 times, 3 hdc in next Puff St, ★ (hdc in next ch-2 sp and in next Puff St) 5 times, skip next ch-1 sp, (hdc in next Puff St and in next ch-2 sp) 5 times, 3 hdc in next Puff St; repeat from ★ across to last 5 Puff Sts, (hdc in next ch-2 sp and in next Puff St) 4 times, YO, insert hook in next ch-2 sp, YO and pull up a loop, YO, insert hook in last Puff St, YO and pull up a loop, YO and draw through all 5 loops on hook, hdc in last hdc: 138 hdc.

Repeat Rows 2-7 until Afghan measures approximately 74", ending by working Row 5.

Finish off.

GRANDMA'S LACE

The elegant ruffles on this mile-a-minute afghan bring to mind the snippets of beautiful lace that could always be found in Grandma's sewing basket. Crocheted in ecru, the eyelet rounds are worked with easy single and double crochet stitches and edged on each side with soft blue.

Finished Size: Approximately 54" x 72"

MATERIALS
Worsted Weight Yarn, approximately:
MC (Blue) - 35 ounces, (990 grams, 2,300 yards)
CC (Ecru) - 27 ounces, (770 grams, 1,775 yards)
Crochet hook, size K (6.50 mm) **or** size needed for gauge
Yarn needle

GAUGE: 14 dc and 7 rows = 4"
One Strip = 3³/4" wide

STRIP (Make 14)
CENTER RUFFLE
With CC, ch 251 **loosely**.
Foundation Row (Right side)**:** Dc in fourth ch from hook and in each ch across: 249 sts.
Note: Loop a short piece of yarn around any stitch to mark last row as **right** side.
Rnd 1: Turn, slip st in first 2 dc, ch 1, turn; sc in same st, ch 4; working in free loops of beginning ch **(Fig. 27b, page 124)**, skip first ch, sc in next ch, (ch 3, skip next ch, sc in next ch) 123 times, ch 4, skip next 3 chs, (sc in next dc, ch 3, skip next dc) around; join with slip st to first sc: 123 ch-3 sps **each** side.
Rnd 2: Slip st in first ch-4 sp, ch 3 **(counts as first dc, now and throughout)**, 4 dc in same sp, 3 dc in next ch-3 sp, (sc in next ch-3 sp, 3 dc in next ch-3 sp) across to next ch-4 sp, 5 dc in ch-4 sp, 3 dc in next ch-3 sp, (sc in next ch-3 sp, 3 dc in next ch-3 sp) around; join with slip st to first dc, finish off.

EDGING
FIRST SIDE
Row 1: With **right** side facing, working in skipped sts on Foundation Row and behind Ruffle (Rnds 1 and 2), join MC with slip st in first st (top of beginning ch); ch 3, dc in same st, 2 dc in next skipped dc and in each skipped st across: 250 dc.
Rows 2 and 3: Ch 3, turn; dc in next dc and in each dc across.
Finish off.

SECOND SIDE
Row 1: With **right** side facing, working in skipped free loops of beginning ch and behind Ruffle (Rnds 1 and 2), join MC with slip st in first ch on Foundation Row; ch 3, dc in same ch, 2 dc in each of next 124 skipped chs: 250 dc.
Rows 2 and 3: Ch 3, turn; dc in next dc and in each dc across.
Finish off.

ASSEMBLY
With **wrong** side of two Strips together and using MC, whipstitch Strips together working in inside loops **(Fig. 29a, page 125)**.
Join remaining Strips in same manner, always working from the same direction.

BORDER
With **right** side of long end facing, join CC with slip st in first dc; ch 2, 3 hdc in same dc, † hdc in next dc and in each dc across to last dc, 4 hdc in last dc; working in end of rows, work 2 hdc in first row and in each row across to corner †, 4 hdc in first dc, repeat from † to † once; join with slip st to top of beginning ch-2, finish off.

NICE FOR THE NURSERY

Looking for something nice for the nursery? This mile-a-minute throw is sized especially for baby, and it works up in a jiffy! Made with sport weight yarn, its soft, delicate pattern is created using simple single and double crochet stitches.

Finished Size: Approximately 33" x 45"

MATERIALS
Sport Weight Yarn, approximately:
  MC (Pink) - 9¼ ounces, (260 grams, 925 yards)
  CC (White) - 4¼ ounces, (120 grams, 425 yards)
Crochet hook, size H (5.00 mm) **or** size needed for gauge

GAUGE: 16 dc and 8 rows = 4"
      One Strip = 3½" wide

Note: To work **Picot**, ch 5, slip st in top of last dc worked.

FIRST STRIP
With MC, ch 168 **loosely.**
Rnd 1 (Right side)**:** Dc in fourth ch from hook, work Picot, (2 dc in same ch, work Picot) twice, dc in same ch, [skip next 3 chs, (3 dc, work Picot, 2 dc) in next ch] across to last 4 chs, skip next 3 chs, (2 dc in last ch, work Picot) 3 times, dc in same ch; working in free loops of beginning ch **(Fig. 27b, page 124)**, skip next 3 chs, [(3 dc, work Picot, 2 dc) in next ch, skip next 3 chs] 40 times; join with slip st to top of beginning ch, finish off: 86 Picots.
Note: Loop a short piece of yarn around any stitch to mark last round as **right** side.
Rnd 2: With **right** side facing, join CC with slip st in any Picot; ch 1, 7 sc in same sp, ch 1, (7 sc in next Picot, ch 1) around; join with slip st to first sc, finish off.
Rnd 3: With **right** side facing and working in center sc of 7-sc groups, join MC with slip st in center sc on either end of Strip; ch 3, dc in same st, † (ch 3, 2 dc in same st) 3 times, 2 dc in next center sc, (ch 3, 2 dc in same st) twice, (2 dc, ch 3, 2 dc) in each of next 40 center sc, 2 dc in next center sc, (ch 3, 2 dc in same st) twice †, 2 dc in next center sc, repeat from † to † once; join with slip st to top of beginning ch-3, finish off.

REMAINING 8 STRIPS
Work same as First Strip through Rnd 2.
Rnd 3 (Joining rnd)**:** With **right** side facing and working in center sc of 7-sc groups, join MC with slip st in center sc on either end of Strip; ch 3, dc in same st, (ch 3, 2 dc in same st) 3 times, 2 dc in next center sc, (ch 3, 2 dc in same st) twice, (2 dc, ch 3, 2 dc) in each of next 40 center sc, 2 dc in next center sc, (ch 3, 2 dc in same st) twice, 2 dc in next center sc, (ch 3, 2 dc in same st) 3 times, (2 dc, ch 3, 2 dc) in next center sc, ch 1, place Strips with **wrong** sides together, slip st in corresponding ch-3 sp on **previous** Strip, ch 1, ★ 2 dc in same sc on **new** Strip, 2 dc in next center sc, ch 1, slip st in next ch-3 sp on **previous** Strip, ch 1; repeat from ★ 40 times **more**, (2 dc, ch 3, 2 dc) in same sc on **new** Strip; join with slip st to top of beginning ch-3, finish off.

EDGING
With **right** side facing, join CC with slip st in any ch-3 sp; ch 1, (sc, hdc, 3 dc, hdc, sc) in same sp and in each ch-3 sp around; join with slip st to first sc, finish off.

LACY TRELLIS

This lacy throw will add a light and airy touch to any decor. Worked holding two strands of yarn together, the afghan features a lovely trellis pattern of shells and double crochet stitches. A lush tasseled fringe completes the feminine look.

Finished Size: Approximately 48" x 70"

MATERIALS

Worsted Weight Yarn, approximately:
    79 ounces, (2,240 grams, 4,610 yards)
Crochet hook, size N (9.00 mm) **or** size needed for
    gauge

Note: Entire Afghan is worked holding two strands of
    yarn together.

GAUGE: 10 dc and 5 rows = 4"

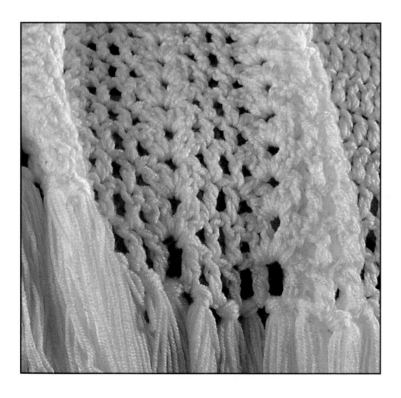

Ch 138 **loosely**.

Row 1 (Right side): Dc in sixth ch from hook, ★ ch 1, skip next ch, dc in next ch; repeat from ★ across: 67 sps.

Note #1: Loop a short piece of yarn around any stitch to mark last row as **right** side.

Note #2: To work **Shell**, (2 dc, ch 2, 2 dc) in sp indicated.

Row 2: Ch 4 (**counts as first dc plus ch 1, now and throughout**), turn; dc in next dc, skip next ch-1 sp, work Shell in next ch-1 sp, skip next ch-1 sp, dc in next dc, (ch 1, dc in next dc, skip next ch-1 sp, work Shell in next ch-1 sp, skip next ch-1 sp, dc in next dc) twice, ★ ch 1, dc in next dc, (dc in next ch-1 sp and in next dc) 5 times, (ch 1, dc in next dc, skip next ch-1 sp, work Shell in next ch-1 sp, skip next ch-1 sp, dc in next dc) 3 times; repeat from ★ 2 times **more**, ch 1, skip next ch, dc in next ch: 12 Shells.

Row 3: Ch 4, turn; (dc in next dc, work Shell in next ch-2 sp, skip next 2 dc, dc in next dc, ch 1) 3 times, ★ dc in next 11 dc, ch 1, (dc in next dc, work Shell in next ch-2 sp, skip next 2 dc, dc in next dc, ch 1) 3 times; repeat from ★ across to last dc, dc in last dc.

Repeat Row 3 until Afghan measures approximately 69", ending by working a **wrong** side row.

Last Row: Ch 4, turn; dc in next dc, (ch 1, skip next dc, dc in next dc, ch 1, dc in next dc) 6 times, ★ ch 1, (skip next dc, dc in next dc, ch 1) 5 times, dc in next dc, (ch 1, skip next dc, dc in next dc, ch 1, dc in next dc) 6 times; repeat from ★ across; finish off: 67 ch-1 sps.

Add fringe across both ends (**Figs. 31a & c, page 126**).

PRETTY IN PINK

This feminine afghan is pretty in pink! For a soft and dreamy look, we blended a strand of ecru brushed acrylic yarn with the pink yarn. A lacy scalloped border lends added charm.

Finished Size: Approximately 45" x 63"

MATERIALS
Worsted Weight Yarn, approximately:
Color A, Basic (Ecru) - 7 ounces,
(200 grams, 460 yards)
Color B, Basic (Pink) - 18 ounces,
(510 grams, 1,185 yards)
Color C, Brushed Acrylic (Ecru) - 23 ounces,
(650 grams, 1,775 yards)
Crochet hook, size N (9.00 mm) **or** size needed for gauge
Yarn needle

Note: Entire Afghan is worked holding one strand of Basic Worsted Weight Yarn and one strand of Brushed Acrylic Worsted Weight Yarn together.

GAUGE: One Motif = 9"

MOTIF (Make 24)
With Color B and Color C, ch 8; join with slip st to form a ring.
Rnd 1 (Right side): Ch 3 (**counts as first dc, now and throughout**), 15 dc in ring; join with slip st to first dc: 16 dc.
Note: Loop a short piece of yarn around any stitch to mark last round as **right** side.
Rnd 2: Ch 4 (**counts as first dc plus ch 1, now and throughout**), (dc in next dc, ch 1) around; join with slip st to first dc: 16 ch-1 sps.
Rnd 3: Ch 3, 2 dc in first ch-1 sp, (dc in next dc, 2 dc in next ch-1 sp) around; join with slip st to first dc: 48 dc.
Rnd 4: Ch 1, sc in same st, ch 5, skip next 2 dc, (sc in next dc, ch 2, skip next 2 dc) 3 times, ★ sc in next dc, ch 5, skip next 2 dc, (sc in next dc, ch 2, skip next 2 dc) 3 times; repeat from ★ around; join with slip st to first sc: 16 sps.
Note: To work **V-St**, (dc, ch 1, dc) in sp indicated.
Rnd 5: Slip st in first corner ch-5 sp, ch 4, (dc, ch 2, work V-St) in same sp, ch 1, (work V-St in next ch-2 sp, ch 1) 3 times, ★ work (V-St, ch 2, V-St) in next corner ch-5 sp, ch 1, (work V-St in next ch-2 sp, ch 1) 3 times; repeat from ★ around; join with slip st to first dc: 20 V-Sts.

Rnd 6: Slip st in first ch-1 sp, slip st in next dc and in next ch-2 sp, ch 4, (dc, ch 2, work V-St) in same sp, ch 1, skip next V-St, (work V-St in next ch-1 sp, ch 1, skip next V-St) 4 times, ★ work (V-St, ch 2, V-St) in next corner ch-2 sp, ch 1, skip next V-St, (work V-St in next ch-1 sp, ch 1, skip next V-St) 4 times; repeat from ★ around; join with slip st to first dc, finish off: 6 V-Sts **each** side.

ASSEMBLY
With **wrong** sides together and using Color B and Color C, whipstitch Motifs together working through inside loops, forming 4 vertical strips of 6 Motifs each (*Fig. 29a, page 125*); then whipstitch strips together.

EDGING
Rnd 1: With **right** side of short end facing and beginning in right corner, join Color A and Color C with slip st in first dc after corner ch-2 sp; ch 1, sc in same st, (sc in next ch-1 sp and in next dc) 11 times, † sc in joining and in first dc of next Motif, (sc in next ch-1 sp and in next dc) 11 times †, repeat from † to † across to next corner ch-2 sp, sc in ch-2 sp, ch 3, ★ sc in next dc, (sc in next ch-1 sp and in next dc) 11 times, repeat from † to † across to next corner ch-2 sp, sc in ch-2 sp, ch 3; repeat from ★ around; join with slip st to first sc: 480 sc.
Rnd 2: Ch 1, sc in same st, ★ † ch 3, skip next 2 sc, sc in next sc, ch 2, skip next sc, sc in next sc, [(ch 3, skip next 2 sc, sc in next sc) twice, ch 2, skip next sc, sc in next sc] across to within 2 sc of next corner ch-3 sp, ch 3, sc in ch-3 sp, ch 3 †, sc in next sc; repeat from ★ 2 times **more**, then repeat from † to † once; join with slip st to first sc: 180 sps.
Note: To work **Shell**, (2 dc, ch 2, 2 dc) in sp indicated.
Rnd 3: Ch 1, sc in same st, ch 2, skip next ch-3 sp, work Shell in next ch-2 sp, ch 2, skip next ch-3 sp, ★ sc in next sc, (ch 2, skip next ch-3 sp, work Shell in next ch-2 sp, ch 2, skip next ch-3 sp, sc in next sc) across to next corner ch-3 sp, ch 3, skip ch-3 sp; repeat from ★ around; join with slip st to first sc: 60 Shells.

Rnd 4: Ch 1, sc in same st, ★ † ch 2, (work Shell in ch-2 sp of next Shell, ch 2, sc in next sc, ch 2) across to next corner ch-3 sp, sc in center ch of corner sp, ch 2 †, sc in next sc; repeat from ★ 2 times **more**, then repeat from † to † once; join with slip st to first sc.

Rnd 5: Ch 1, sc in same st, ★ † ch 2, [(2 dc, ch 3, 2 dc) in ch-2 sp of next Shell, ch 2, sc in next sc, ch 2] across to next corner sc, dc in corner sc, ch 2 †, sc in next sc; repeat from ★ 2 times **more**, then repeat from † to † once; join with slip st to first sc.

Rnd 6: Ch 1, sc in same st, ★ † (ch 4, 5 dc in next ch-3 sp, ch 4, sc in next sc) across to next corner dc, ch 3, dc in corner dc, ch 3 †, sc in next sc; repeat from ★ 2 times **more**, then repeat from † to † once; join with slip st to first sc, finish off.

SLEEPY SHELLS

Gather up this sweet afghan when it's time to send baby off to dreamland! It's made with worsted weight brushed acrylic yarn for a soft, cozy texture. Because the alternating rows of pretty blue shells and delicate white eyelet are worked using simple crochet stitches, you can complete our nap-time throw in no time.

Finished Size: Approximately 34½" x 45"

MATERIALS
Worsted Weight Brushed Acrylic Yarn,
  approximately:
    MC (Blue) - 14 ounces,
      (400 grams, 885 yards)
    CC (White) - 11 ounces,
      (310 grams, 700 yards)
Crochet hook, size H (5.00 mm) **or** size needed for
  gauge

GAUGE: 3 Sleepy Shells = 4"

With CC, ch 154 **loosely**.
Row 1 (Right side): Dc in sixth ch from hook, ★ ch 1, skip next ch, dc in next ch; repeat from ★ across changing to MC in last dc (**Fig. 28, page 124**): 75 sps.

Note: Loop a short piece of yarn around any stitch to mark last row as **right** side.
Row 2: Ch 1, turn; sc in first dc, ch 1, (sc in next dc, ch 1) across, skip next ch, sc in next ch.
Note: To work **Sleepy Shell**, dc in next ch-1 sp, ch 3, work 3 dc around post of dc just made (**Fig. 24, page 123**).
Row 3: Ch 3, turn; ★ skip next ch-1 sp, work Sleepy Shell in next ch-1 sp, skip next sc, dc in next sc; repeat from ★ across changing to CC in last dc: 25 Sleepy Shells.
Row 4: Ch 5, turn; skip next 3 dc, sc in top of next ch-3, ch 2, ★ dc in next dc, ch 2, skip next 3 dc, sc in top of next ch-3, ch 2; repeat from ★ across, dc in top of last ch-3: 50 sps.
Row 5: Ch 4, turn; (dc in next sp, ch 1) twice, ★ dc in next dc, ch 1, (dc in next sp, ch 1) twice; repeat from ★ across, dc in third ch of turning ch changing to MC in last dc: 75 sps.
Repeat Rows 2-5 until Afghan measures approximately 43½", ending by working Row 5; do **not** change to MC at end of last row.

EDGING
Rnd 1: Ch 1, do **not** turn; work 193 sc evenly spaced across end of rows; working in free loops of beginning ch (**Fig. 27b, page 124**), 3 sc in first ch, 2 sc in next ch, sc in next 147 chs, 2 sc in next ch, 3 sc in next ch; work 193 sc evenly spaced across end of rows; working across sts of last row, 3 sc in third ch of beginning ch, 2 sc in first ch-1 sp, sc in each dc and in each ch-1 sp across to last ch-1 sp, 2 sc in last ch-1 sp, 3 sc in last dc; join with slip st to first sc, finish off: 700 sc.
Rnd 2: With **right** side facing, join MC with slip st in any corner sc; ch 3, 4 dc in same st, skip next sc, sc in next sc, (skip next 2 sc, 5 dc in next sc, skip next 2 sc, sc in next sc) across to within one sc of next corner sc, ★ 5 dc in corner sc, skip next sc, sc in next sc, (skip next 2 sc, 5 dc in next sc, skip next 2 sc, sc in next sc) across to within one sc of next corner sc; repeat from ★ around; join with slip st to top of beginning ch-3, finish off.

GENERAL INSTRUCTIONS

YARN

Yarn listed under Materials for each afghan in this book is given in a generic weight. Once you know the weight of the yarn, any brand of the same weight may be used. This enables you to purchase the brand of yarn you like best.

You may wish to purchase a single skein first and crochet a gauge swatch. Compare the way your yarn looks to the photograph to be sure that you will be satisfied with the results. How many skeins to buy depends on the yardage. Ounces and grams will vary from one brand of the same weight to another, but the **yardage** required will always remain the same provided gauge is met and maintained.

GAUGE

Correct gauge is essential for proper size. Hook sizes given in instructions are merely guides and should never be used without first making a sample swatch in the stitch, yarn, and hook specified. Then measure it, counting your stitches and rows carefully. If your swatch is smaller than specified, try again with a larger size hook; if larger, try again with a smaller size. Keep trying until you find the size that will give you the specified gauge. DO NOT HESITATE TO CHANGE HOOK SIZE TO OBTAIN CORRECT GAUGE.

ABBREVIATIONS

BB	Blackberry stitch
BLO	Back Loop(s) Only
BPtr	Back Post treble crochet(s)
CC	Contrasting Color
ch(s)	chain(s)
dc	double crochet(s)
dtr	double treble crochet(s)
FPdc	Front Post double crochet(s)
FPdtr	Front Post double treble crochet(s)
FPtr	Front Post treble crochet(s)
hdc	half double crochet(s)
LDC	Long Double Crochet(s)
MC	Main Color
mm	millimeters
Rnd(s)	Round(s)
sc	single crochet(s)
sp(s)	space(s)
st(s)	stitch(es)
tr	treble crochet(s)
YO	yarn over

★ — work instructions following ★ as many **more** times as indicated in addition to the first time.

† to † — work all instructions from first † to second † **as many** times as specified.

( ) or [ ] — work enclosed instructions **as many** times as specified by the number immediately following **or** work all enclosed instructions in the stitch or space indicated **or** contains explanatory remarks.

BASIC STITCH GUIDE

CHAIN

When beginning a first row of crochet in a chain, always skip the first chain from the hook, and work into the second chain from hook (for single crochet) or third chain from hook (for half double crochet), etc. (*Fig. 1*).

Fig. 1

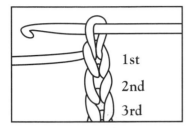

WORKING INTO THE CHAIN

Method #1: Insert hook under top two strands of each chain (*Fig. 2a*).
Method #2: Insert hook in back ridge of each chain (*Fig. 2b*).

Fig. 2a

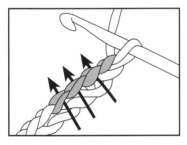

Fig. 2b

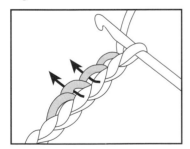

SLIP STITCH

Insert hook in stitch or space indicated, YO and draw through stitch **and** loop on hook (*Fig. 3*) (**slip stitch made,** *abbreviated slip st*).

Fig. 3

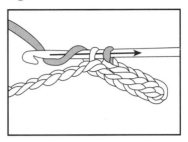

SINGLE CROCHET

Insert hook in stitch or space indicated, YO and pull up a loop, (2 loops on hook) YO and draw through both loops on hook (*Fig. 4*) (**single crochet made,** *abbreviated sc*).

Fig. 4

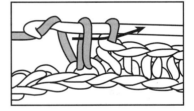

HALF DOUBLE CROCHET

YO, insert hook in stitch or space indicated, YO and pull up a loop (3 loops on hook), YO and draw through all 3 loops on hook (*Fig. 5*) (**half double crochet made,** *abbreviated hdc*).

Fig. 5

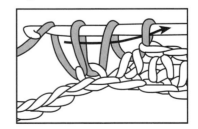

DOUBLE CROCHET

YO, insert hook in stitch or space indicated, YO and pull up a loop (3 loops on hook), YO and draw through 2 loops on hook *(Fig. 6a)*, YO and draw through remaining 2 loops on hook *(Fig. 6b)* (double crochet made, *abbreviated dc*).

Fig. 6a

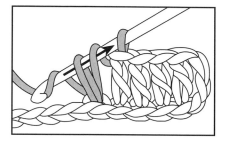

Fig. 6b

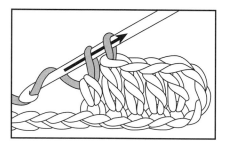

TREBLE CROCHET

YO twice, insert hook in stitch or space indicated, YO and pull up a loop (4 loops on hook) *(Fig. 7a)*, (YO and draw through 2 loops on hook) 3 times *(Fig. 7b)* (treble crochet made, *abbreviated tr*).

Fig. 7a

Fig. 7b

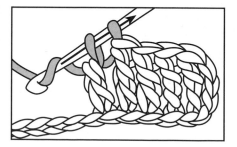

DOUBLE TREBLE CROCHET

YO three times, insert hook in stitch or space indicated, YO and pull up a loop (5 loops on hook) *(Fig. 8a)*, (YO and draw through 2 loops on hook) 4 times *(Fig. 8b)* (double treble crochet made, *abbreviated dtr*).

Fig. 8a

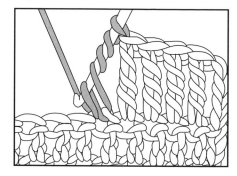

Fig. 8b

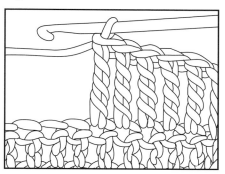

PATTERN STITCHES

POPCORN

Work number of dc specified in stitch or space indicated, drop loop from hook, insert hook in first dc of dc group, hook dropped loop and draw through *(Figs. 9a & b)*.

Fig. 9a   5-dc Popcorn

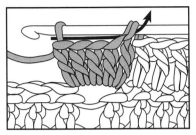

Fig. 9b   4-dc Popcorn

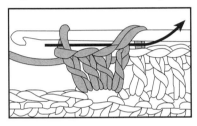

POST STITCH

Work around post of stitch indicated, inserting hook in direction of arrow *(Fig. 10)*.

Fig. 10

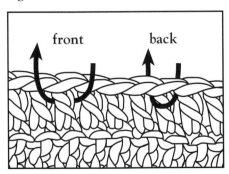

FRONT POST DOUBLE CROCHET

YO, insert hook from **front** to **back** around post of stitch indicated, YO and pull up a loop (3 loops on hook) *(Fig. 11)*, (YO and draw through 2 loops on hook) twice **(Front Post double crochet made, *abbreviated FPdc)*.

Fig. 11

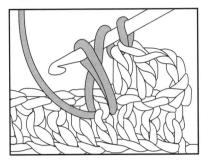

FRONT POST TREBLE CROCHET

YO twice, insert hook from **front** to **back** around post of stitch indicated, YO and pull up a loop (4 loops on hook) *(Fig. 12)*, (YO and draw through 2 loops on hook) 3 times **(Front Post treble crochet made, *abbreviated FPtr)*.

Fig. 12

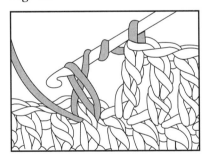

FRONT POST DOUBLE TREBLE CROCHET

YO 3 times, insert hook from **front** to **back** around post of stitch indicated, YO and pull up a loop (5 loops on hook) *(Fig. 13)*, (YO and draw through 2 loops on hook) 4 times **(Front Post double treble made,** *abbreviated FPdtr)*.

Fig. 13

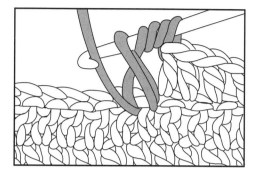

BACK POST TREBLE CROCHET

YO twice, insert hook from **back** to **front** around post of stitch indicated, YO and pull up a loop (4 loops on hook) *(Fig. 14)*, (YO and draw through 2 loops on hook) 3 times **(Back Post treble crochet made,** *abbreviated BPtr)*.

Fig. 14

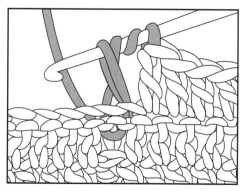

FLOWER PATCH PLACEMENT CHART

Fig. 15

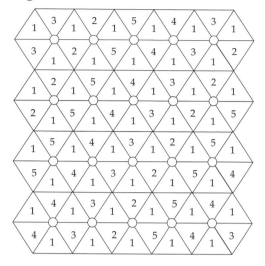

STAR MOTIF

With MC, ch 4; join with slip st to form a ring, ch 1, sc in ring, ch 2, with **right** side facing and working in intersection of 6 Motifs, slip st in any joining, ch 2, ★ sc in ring, ch 2, slip st in next joining, ch 2; repeat from ★ 4 times **more**; join with slip st to first sc *(Fig. 16)*, finish off.

Fig. 16

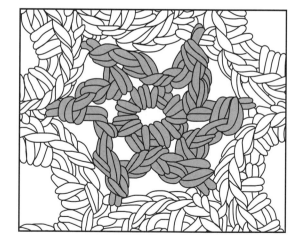

REVERSE SINGLE CROCHET

Working from **left** to **right**, insert hook in stitch to right of hook *(Fig. 17a)*, YO and draw through, under and to left of loop on hook (2 loops on hook) *(Fig. 17b)*, YO and draw through both loops on hook *(Fig. 17c)* **(reverse sc made, *Fig. 17d*)**.

Fig. 17a

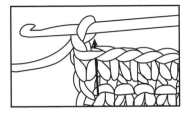

Fig. 17b

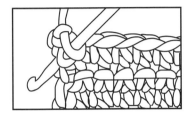

Fig. 17c

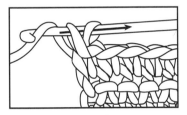

Fig. 17d

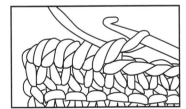

REVERSE HALF DOUBLE CROCHET

YO, working from **left** to **right**, insert hook in stitch or space indicated to right of hook *(Fig. 18a)*, YO and draw through, under and to left of loops on hook (3 loops on hook) *(Fig. 18b)*, YO and draw through all 3 loops on hook *(Fig. 18c)* **(reverse hdc made, *Fig. 18d*)**.

Fig. 18a

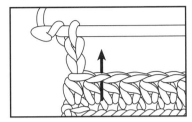

Fig. 18b

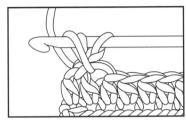

Fig. 18c

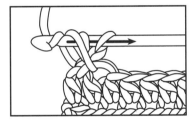

Fig. 18d

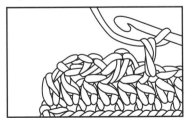

LONG DOUBLE CROCHET

YO, insert hook in next ch-1 space 2 rows **below** *(Fig. 19)*, YO and pull up a loop even with hook, (YO and draw through 2 loops on hook) twice (**Long double crochet made**, *abbreviated LDC*).

Fig. 19

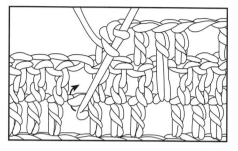

HORIZONTAL STRAND

YO, insert hook in horizontal strand of dc *(Fig. 20)* and pull up a loop, (YO and draw through 2 loops on hook) twice.

Fig. 20

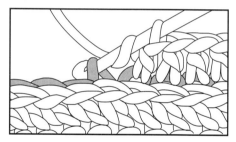

CROSS STITCH

Skip next 2 dc, dc in next 2 dc *(Fig. 21a)*, dc in first skipped dc *(Fig. 21b)* and in next skipped dc.

Fig. 21a

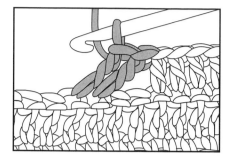

Fig. 21b

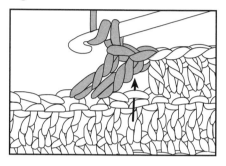

PUFF STITCH

(YO, insert hook in stitch indicated, YO and pull up a loop even with stitch on hook) 3 times, YO and draw through all 7 loops on hook *(Fig. 22)*.

Fig. 22

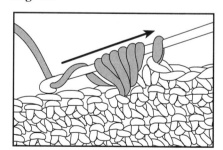

CHAIN CABLE

Ch 3 **loosely**, skip next 2 dc, sc in next dc *(Fig. 23a)*, **turn**; sc in each ch just completed *(Fig. 23b)*, slip st in next sc (sc before ch was begun) *(Fig. 23c)*, **turn**; working **behind** ch-3, sc in each of 2 skipped dc *(Fig. 23d)*.

Fig. 23a

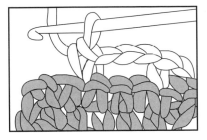

Fig. 23b

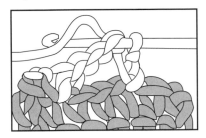

Fig. 23c

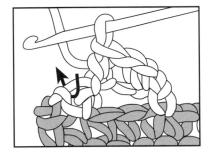

Fig. 23d

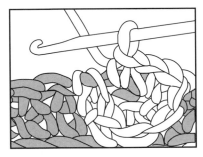

SLEEPY SHELL

Dc in next ch-1 sp, ch 3, work 3 dc around post of dc just made *(Fig. 24)*.

Fig. 24

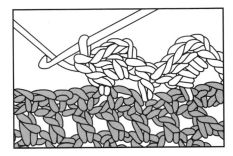

STITCHING TIPS

BEGINNING LOOP

Leaving a 3" end, wind yarn around finger once to form a ring, insert hook in ring, YO and pull up a loop *(Fig. 25)*.

Fig. 25

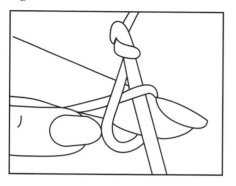

BACK OR FRONT LOOP ONLY

Work only in loop(s) indicated by arrow *(Fig. 26)*.

Fig. 26

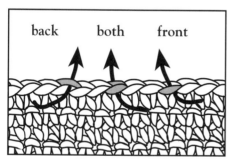

FREE LOOPS

After working in Back or Front Loops Only on a row or round, there will be a ridge of unused loops. These are called the free loops. Later, when instructed to work in the free loops of the same row or round, work in these loops *(Fig. 27a)*.

When instructed to work in free loops of a beginning chain, work in loop indicated by arrow *(Fig. 27b)*.

Fig. 27a

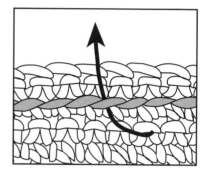

Fig. 27b

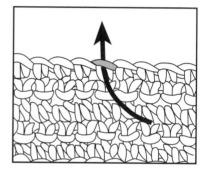

CHANGING COLORS

Work the last stitch to within one step of completion, hook new yarn *(Fig. 28)* and draw through all loops on hook. Cut old yarn and work over both ends, unless otherwise specified.

Fig. 28

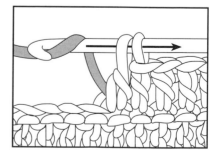

FINISHING

WHIPSTITCH

With **wrong** sides together and beginning in corner stitch, sew through both pieces once to secure the beginning of the seam, leaving an ample yarn end to weave in later. Insert the needle from **right** to **left** through **inside** loops of each piece *(Fig. 29a)* or through **both** loops *(Fig. 29b)*. Bring the needle around and insert it from **right** to **left** through the next loops of **both** pieces. Repeat along the edge, keeping the sewing yarn fairly loose and being careful to match stitches and/or rows.

Fig. 29a

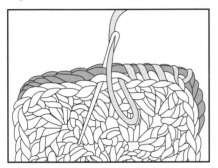

Fig. 29b

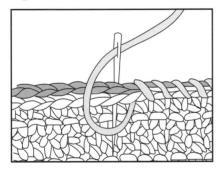

TASSEL

Cut a piece of cardboard 3" wide and as long as you want your finished tassel to be. Wind a double strand of yarn around the cardboard approximately 20 times. Cut an 18" length of yarn and insert it under all the strands at the top of the cardboard; pull up **tightly** and tie securely. Leave the yarn ends long enough to attach the tassel. Cut the yarn at the opposite end of the cardboard *(Fig. 30a)* and then remove it. Cut a 6" length of yarn and wrap it **tightly** around the tassel twice, $1/2$" below the top *(Fig. 30b)*; tie securely. Trim the ends.

Fig. 30a

Fig. 30b

FRINGE

Cut a piece of cardboard 3" wide and ½" longer than you want your finished fringe to be. Wind the yarn **loosely** and **evenly** around the cardboard until the card is filled, then cut across one end; repeat as needed.

Hold together half as many strands of yarn as desired for the finished fringe; fold in half. With **wrong** side facing and using a crochet hook, draw the folded end up through a stitch or space and pull the loose ends through the folded end *(Figs. 31a & b)*; draw the knot up tightly *(Figs. 31c & d)*. Repeat, spacing as desired. Lay flat on a hard surface and trim the ends.

Fig. 31a

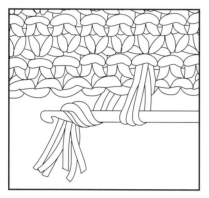

Fig. 31b

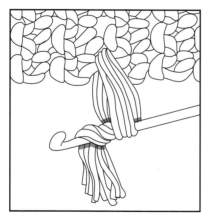

Fig. 31c

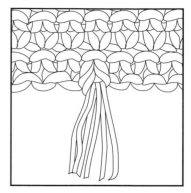

Fig. 31d

126

CREDITS

To Magna IV Color Imaging of Little Rock, Arkansas, we say thank you for the superb color reproduction and excellent pre-press preparation.

We want to especially thank photographers Ken West, Larry Pennington, and Mark Mathews of Peerless Photography, Little Rock, Arkansas, and Jerry R. Davis of Jerry Davis Photography, Little Rock, Arkansas, for their time, patience, and excellent work.

We would like to extend a special word of thanks to the talented designers who created the lovely projects in this book:

Eleanor Albano, Inc., for Alexander-Stratton Designs, Inc.: *Herb Garden*, page 10; *Spring Throw*, page 18; *Cobblestones*, page 30; *Peaches & Cream*, page 34; and *Distinctive Design*, page 84

Mary Lamb Becker: *White Lace*, page 96

Carol Brill: *Filet Diamonds*, page 86

Ginna Brizendine: *Painted Desert*, page 40

Anne Halliday: *Shades of the Sea*, page 46

Jan Hatfield: *Berry Basket*, page 24; *Country Lane*, page 28; *Primary Fun*, page 60; *Rose Rhapsody*, page 94; and *Grandma's Lace*, page 106

Jeneel Johnson: *Merry and Bright*, page 58, and *Understated Elegance*, page 70

Shala Johnson: *Color It Easy*, page 44

Terry Kimbrough: *All-American Afghan*, page 8; *Cozy Wrap*, page 26; *Sunny and Warm*, page 52; *Victorian Heirloom*, page 68; *Soft Stripes*, page 76; *Lacy Shells*, page 88; *Timeless Flowers*, page 90; *Rosebuds*, page 100; and *Lacy Trellis*, page 110

Jennine Korejko: *Rock-A-Bye Wrap*, page 102, and *Nice for the Nursery*, page 108

Carole Prior: *True Blue*, page 56, and *Keepsake Cover-up*, page 98

Mary Jane Protus: *Heather Lace*, page 80, and *Sleepy Shells*, page 114

Carole Rutter Tippett: *Lacy Blocks*, page 6; *Plain and Simple*, page 12; *Flower Patch*, page 14; *Country Fisherman*, page 16; *Fields of Green*, page 22; *Blue and White Favorite*, page 32; *Plush Polka Dots*, page 36; *Campus Colors*, page 54; *The Red, White, and Blue*, page 62; *Sophisticated Swirl*, page 66; *Precious Pearls*, page 72; *Lovely Ripples*, page 74; *Classic Texture*, page 78; *Elegant Harmony*, page 82; *Vintage Ripple*, page 104; and *Pretty in Pink*, page 112

Joyce Winfield Vanderslice: *Really Red*, page 50

We extend a sincere *thank you* to the people who assisted in making and testing many of the projects in this book: Judy Crowder, Lee Ellis, Naomi Greening, Raymelle Greening, Pat Little, Bill Tanner, and Sherry Williams.